# Contents

Tables

Figures

# GAO

Report to the Chairman, Subcommittee on Oversight of Government Management, the Federal Workforce, and the District of Columbia, Committee on Homeland Security and Governmental Affairs, U.S. Senate

February 2012

# BACKGROUND INVESTIGATIONS

# Office of Personnel Management Needs to Improve Transparency of Its Pricing and Seek Cost Savings

**GAO**
Accountability ★ Integrity ★ Reliability

# BACKGROUND INVESTIGATIONS

## Office of Personnel Management Needs to Improve Transparency of Its Pricing and Seek Cost Savings

**G A O**

Accountability * Integrity * Reliability

# Highlights

Highlights of GAO-12-197, a report to the Chairman, Subcommittee on Oversight of Government Management, the Federal Workforce, and the District of Columbia, Committee on Homeland Security and Governmental Affairs, U.S. Senate

## Why GAO Did This Study

In fiscal year 2011, the Office of Personnel Management (OPM), as the investigative service provider for most of the federal government, received over $1 billion to conduct more than 2 million background investigations (suitability determinations and personnel security clearances) for government employees. The 2004 Intelligence Reform and Terrorism Prevention Act and the resulting governmentwide reform (led by the Performance Accountability Council) helped to improve the timeliness and quality of investigations. GAO was asked to (1) identify the cost trends related to OPM's background investigations since fiscal year 2005 and the principal factors driving OPM's costs, (2) assess how OPM develops the background investigation prices it charges to agencies and the extent to which the basis of these prices is transparent, and (3) assess the extent to which governmentwide reform efforts have focused on reducing costs. For this review, GAO analyzed OPM's reported background investigation cost, workload and pricing data from fiscal years 2005 to 2011; examined key background investigation reform effort documents; and conducted interviews with executive branch agencies' officials.

## What GAO Recommends

GAO recommends that OPM provide customer agencies better information on the costs of background investigations and identify and address efficiencies that could lead to cost savings. GAO also recommends that the Office of Management and Budget (OMB), through the Performance Accountability Council, expand its reform focus to identify opportunities for cost savings. OPM and OMB concurred; however, OPM raised issues with the basis of some of GAO's findings. GAO disagrees and addresses these issues in this report.

View GAO-12-197. For more information, contact Brenda S. Farrell at (202) 512-3604 or farrellb@gao.gov.

## What GAO Found

OPM's reported costs to conduct background investigations increased by almost 79 percent, from about $602 million in fiscal year 2005 to almost $1.1 billion in fiscal year 2011 (in fiscal year 2011 dollars). However, the extent to which OPM's cost data are reliable is unknown because an audit of OPM's revolving fund, which finances business-type operations, has not been conducted. Independent audits of OPM's overall financial management system, where revolving fund transactions are recorded, identified material weaknesses in internal controls, which could affect the reliability of these cost data. OPM's background investigation program has three principal cost drivers. The first cost driver is investigation fieldwork and support contracts, which represent nearly half of OPM's fiscal year 2011 reported costs—about $532 million. These contracts allow OPM to assign an investigation to a contractor and buy clerical support for case-management. The second cost driver is personnel compensation and benefits for OPM's background investigation federal workforce, which represents about 25 percent of OPM's fiscal year 2011 reported costs—about $265 million. The third cost driver is OPM's information technology investments. While these investments represent less than 10 percent of fiscal year 2011 reported costs, they have increased more than 682 percent over 6 years (in fiscal year 2011 dollars), from about $12 million in fiscal year 2005 to over $91 million in fiscal year 2011. OPM attributed cost increases to more comprehensive subject interviews, increased FBI fees, and compliance with investigation timeliness requirements.

OPM develops prices for background investigations using aggregated operating costs and does not provide customer agencies with transparent information underlying its prices and price increases. Customer agency officials expressed dissatisfaction that OPM does not provide more transparent information about how it derived its prices. According to previous GAO work on the management of revolving funds and user fees, agencies should provide their program information to customer agencies, stakeholders, and Congress, to help ensure transparency of costs. Given the lack of transparency underlying the prices and price increases, some agencies believe they may be overcharged and are looking into alternative means for carrying out their investigations, which could lead to duplication that is contrary to the goals of the governmentwide suitability and personnel security clearance reform effort. OPM has information regarding its aggregated operating costs, including federal personnel costs and information technology investments, that could improve customers' understanding of how OPM determines its prices if shared.

Governmentwide suitability and personnel security clearance reform efforts have not yet focused on cost savings. The stated mission of these efforts includes improving cost savings, timeliness, and quality, among others. While the Performance Accountability Council has focused on improving timeliness and quality, it has not provided the executive branch with guidance on cost savings. However, GAO identified opportunities for achieving cost savings or cost avoidance. Specifically, agencies have made duplicative investments in case-management and adjudication systems without considering opportunities for leveraging existing technologies. Further, OPM's investigation process has not been studied for process efficiencies that could lead to cost savings. In addition, OPM invested in an electronic case-management program yet continues to convert submitted electronic files to paper. Given the pressure government agencies are under to reduce costs, the Performance Accountability Council, including OPM, is well-positioned to identify opportunities for cost savings within the process.

_____ **United States Government Accountability Office**

## Abbreviations

| | |
|---|---|
| OPM | Office of Personnel Management |
| DOD | Department of Defense |
| IRTPA | Intelligence Reform and Terrorism Prevention Act |
| FBI | Federal Bureau of Investigation |

United States Government Accountability Office
Washington, DC 20548

February 28, 2012

The Honorable Daniel K. Akaka
Chairman
Subcommittee on Oversight of Government Management, the Federal
   Workforce, and the District of Columbia
Committee on Homeland Security and Governmental Affairs
United States Senate

Dear Mr. Chairman,

The federal government spent over $1 billion to conduct more than 2 million background investigations (in support of suitability determinations and personnel security clearances) for government employment outside the Intelligence Community in fiscal year 2011.[1] The Office of Personnel Management (OPM) is currently the investigative service provider for the majority of the federal government, and all of this work is conducted by its Federal Investigative Services division. The Department of Defense (DOD) is OPM's largest customer, and the recipient of over 788,000 background investigations that cost over $787 million in fiscal year 2011.[2] OPM's charges to DOD for these investigation requests constituted about 74 percent of OPM Federal Investigative Services' total revenue in fiscal year 2011.

In our biennial High-Risk series, we first designated the DOD personnel security clearance program a high-risk area in 2005 because of delays in administering the program and resulting backlogs of clearance

---

[1]Determinations of suitability for government employment in positions in the competitive service and for career appointment in the Senior Executive Service include consideration of aspects of an individual's character or conduct that may have an effect on the integrity or efficiency of their service. Personnel security clearances allow government and industry personnel to gain access to classified information that, through unauthorized disclosure, can in some cases cause exceptionally grave damage to U.S. national security.

[2]This number is based on DOD data and represents stand-alone investigations that OPM conducted for DOD in 2011. For purposes of this report, we define stand-alone investigations as those that result in a suitability determination, secret, or top secret clearance.

GAO-12-197 Background Investigations

investigations.[3] Just prior to our designation, Congress set objectives and established requirements for reforming the clearance process in section 3001 of the Intelligence Reform and Terrorism Prevention Act (IRTPA) of 2004 in light of long-standing concerns regarding delays in processing clearances and other issues.[4] IRTPA established objectives for timeliness, requirements for reciprocity (i.e., that, subject to certain exceptions, all agencies shall accept a background investigation or clearance determination completed by any other authorized investigative or adjudicative agency), and an integrated, secure database to house clearance information.

To improve the process related to determining suitability for government employment and granting security clearances and to achieve established timeliness goals, in 2007, the Director of National Intelligence and Under Secretary of Defense for Intelligence formed the Security Clearance Process Reform Team or Joint Reform Team. The Suitability and Security Clearance Performance Accountability Council (Performance Accountability Council) was later formed to oversee agency progress in implementing the reform vision,[5] and is chaired by the Deputy Director for Management of the Office of Management and Budget and vice-chaired by DOD. The council—which is led by the Office of Management and Budget, DOD, Office of the Director of National Intelligence, and OPM and currently comprises representatives from 10 other executive-branch agencies[6]—released several reports detailing reform-related plans, including a strategic framework in February 2010 that establishes goals, performance measures, roles and responsibilities, and proposed metrics for determining the quality of security clearance investigations and adjudications.[7] However, the strategic framework did not contain details

---

[3]GAO, *High-Risk Series: An Update,* GAO-05-207 (Washington, D.C.: January 2005).

[4]Pub. L. No. 108-458 (2004) (codified at 50 U.S.C. § 435b).

[5]Exec. Order No. 13467, *Reforming Processes Related to Suitability for Government Employment, Fitness for Contractor Employees, and Eligibility for Access to Classified National Security Information,* § 2.2 (June 30, 2008).

[6]The Performance Accountability Council includes the Office of Management and Budget (Chair), Office of the Director of National Intelligence, Office of Personnel Management, DOD (Vice-chair), Department of State, Federal Bureau of Investigation (FBI), Department of Homeland Security, Department of Energy, Department of Health and Human Services, Department of Veterans Affairs, and Department of the Treasury.

[7]Performance Accountability Council, *Security and Suitability Process Reform Strategic Framework* (Washington, D.C.: February 2010).

about the funding requirements of reform, the cost of background investigations governmentwide, or cost savings that may result from reform. In 2011, we removed DOD's personnel security clearance program from the high-risk list as a result of DOD's commitment to sustaining progress in timeliness and quality, as well as its demonstrated progress in meeting IRTPA timeliness objectives.[8] Figure 1 below describes these and other events related to suitability and security clearance reform over the past decade.

**Figure 1: Key Events Related to the Suitability and Personnel Security Clearance Reform Effort**

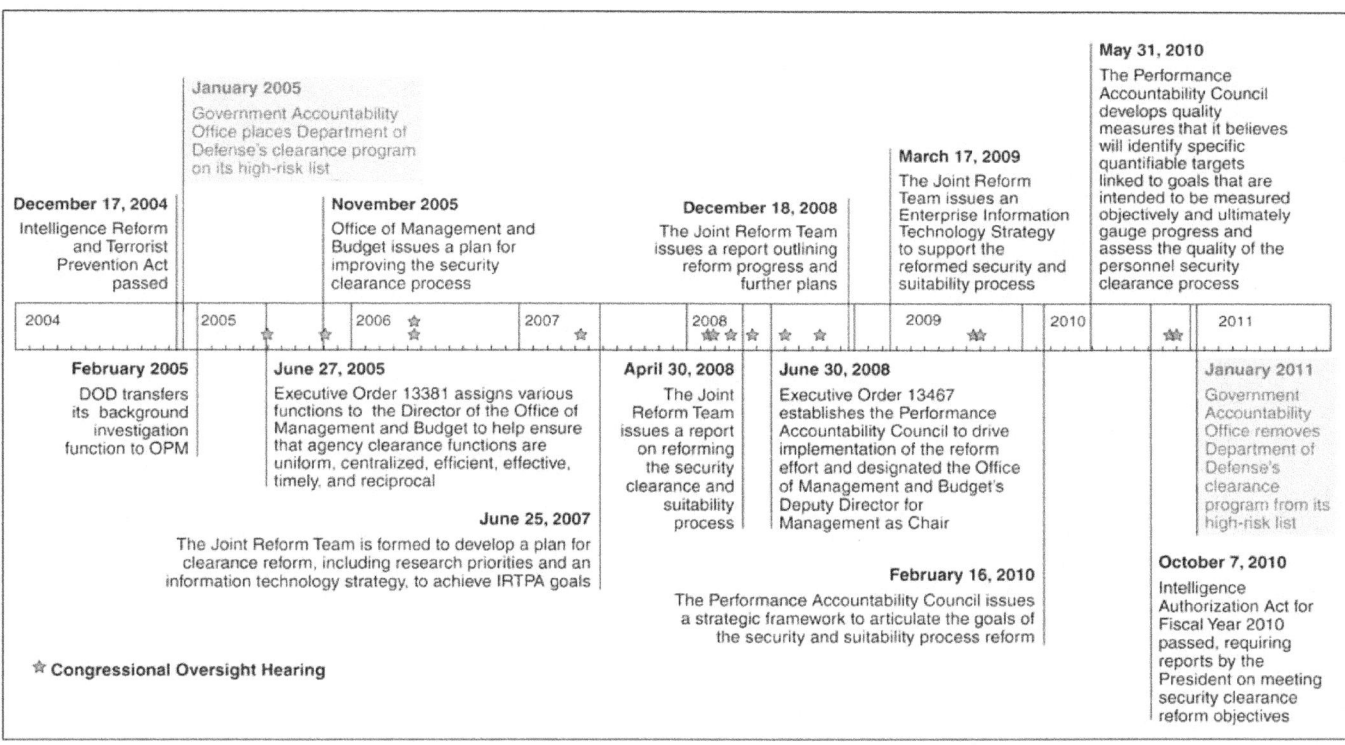

Source: GAO analysis.

You requested that we conduct a review of the OPM Federal Investigative

---

[8]GAO, *High-Risk Series: An Update,* GAO-07-310 (Washington, D.C.: January 2007); *High-Risk Series: An Update,* GAO-09-271 (Washington, D.C.: January 2009); and *High-Risk Series: An Update,* GAO-11-278 (Washington, D.C.: February 2011).

Services' pricing model to determine the actual costs attributable to all aspects of the various investigative products and packages. Specifically, we (1) identified the cost trends related to OPM's background investigations since fiscal year 2005 and determined the principal factors driving OPM's costs, (2) assessed how OPM develops the background investigation prices charged to agencies and the extent to which the basis of these prices is transparent, and (3) assessed the extent to which governmentwide reform efforts have focused on reducing costs.

This report examines background investigations for security clearances and suitability determinations that are performed by OPM's federal workforce and investigative contractors, and OPM's relationship with its customer agencies. In addition to OPM, we met with representatives from DOD and five additional executive branch agencies that use OPM to conduct background investigations for their employees.[9] We also met with three DOD intelligence agencies that have authority to conduct their own investigations to understand their processes and costs. We relied on OPM's reported cost data for the purposes of our report; however, the extent to which these data are reliable is unknown because an audit of OPM's revolving fund[10] has not been conducted. Nonetheless, independent audits of OPM's overall financial management system, where revolving fund transactions are recorded, identified material weaknesses in internal controls, and these weaknesses could affect the reliability of the cost data. Those audits also made recommendations to OPM to correct the material weaknesses. Even so, these are the only Federal Investigative Services' cost data available, and OPM relies on them to identify its annual operating costs. For our first objective, to identify cost trends related to OPM's background investigations since fiscal year 2005 and determine the principal factors driving OPM costs, we obtained and analyzed Federal Investigative Services' reported direct

---

[9]For a complete list of agencies interviewed in support of this review, see tables 5 and 6 in app. I.

[10]An intragovernmental revolving fund is an appropriation account authorized to be credited with collections from other federal agencies' accounts that are earmarked to finance a continuing cycle of business-type operations. According to the Office of Management and Budget, collections of intragovernmental revolving fund accounts are derived primarily from within the government. GAO, *A Glossary of Terms Used in the Federal Budget Process*, GAO-05-734SP (Washington, D.C.: September 2005.) The self-sustaining nature of these accounts means that funds received in exchange for services remains available for authorized purposes without needing to be reappropriated, subject to certain conditions.

and indirect costs, revenues, and expenses from fiscal years 2005 through 2011.[11] Further, we interviewed knowledgeable OPM officials from offices responsible for overseeing budgetary records and discussed OPM's budgetary processes and procedures related to background investigations. For our second objective, to assess how OPM develops the background investigation prices charged to agencies and the extent to which the basis of these prices is transparent, we reviewed (1) OPM's pricing standard operating procedure and related documentation; (2) annual investigation pricing rates established by Federal Investigative Services; (3) fieldwork and investigation support contracts; (4) transaction processes between OPM and selected executive branch customer agencies;[12] and (5) OPM and customer interagency agreements, which serve as an official record of the amounts transferred between the agencies for investigative services. We interviewed knowledgeable officials from related OPM divisions, including Federal Investigative Services (Technical Services, Customer Services, and Business Management) and the Chief Financial Office; three private investigative firms that contract with OPM; selected OPM customer agencies—including DOD—that have the six largest annual transactions with OPM;[13]

---

[11]We define cost drivers as factors that influence or contribute to the expense of business operations, and in this case the operation is OPM Federal Investigative Services' background investigations program. According to the Federal Accounting Standards Advisory Board, direct costs are costs that can be specifically identified with an output. All direct costs should be included in the full cost of outputs. Typical direct costs in the production of an output include (a) salaries and other benefits for employees who work directly on the output; (b) materials and supplies used in the work; (c) various costs associated with office space, equipment, facilities, and utilities that are used exclusively to produce the output; and (d) costs of goods or services received from other segments or entities that are used to produce the output. Indirect costs are costs of resources that are jointly or commonly used to produce two or more types of outputs but are not specifically identifiable with any of the outputs. Typical examples of indirect costs include rent, and operating and maintenance costs for buildings, equipment, and utilities, among others. Some costs can be either indirect or direct. For example, OPM classifies its training expenses as both direct (such as training for field contractors) and indirect (such as training associated with Federal Investigative Services' federal personnel).

[12]We met with officials from DOD and the Departments of Energy, Justice, the Treasury, Homeland Security, and Veterans Affairs. We selected agencies on the basis of their ability to meet a combination of one or more of the following criteria: (1) utilizes OPM to conduct most of its security clearance investigations, (2) ranks among OPM's top 10 largest investigation customers, by volume or by total expenditures in fiscal year 2010; and (3) is a member of the Performance Accountability Council. Because this is a nonprobability sample, our findings do not generalize to the agencies that we did not include in our review.

[13]Ibid.

and three agencies from DOD's Intelligence Community that conduct their own investigations for comparison purposes. For our third objective, to assess the extent to which governmentwide efforts have focused on reducing costs, we analyzed various Performance Accountability Council and Joint Reform Team documents, including reform strategic plans and information on technology initiatives within the investigative process; reviewed internal OPM reports regarding its background investigation process and information technology initiatives, and met with officials from the Intelligence Community, selected OPM customer agencies, and three private investigative firms. We also interviewed knowledgeable officials from OPM, DOD, and Office of the Director of National Intelligence to understand the status of reform initiatives and determine the extent to which cost analyses of these initiatives have been conducted.

We conducted this performance audit from March 2011 through February 2012 in accordance with generally accepted government auditing standards. Those standards require that we plan and perform the audit to obtain sufficient, appropriate evidence to provide a reasonable basis for our findings and conclusions based on our audit objectives. We believe that the evidence obtained provides a reasonable basis for our findings and conclusions based on our audit objectives. Appendix I describes our scope and methodology in more detail.

## Background

OPM provides background investigations for suitability determinations and personnel security clearances to agencies governmentwide. OPM's Federal Investigative Services provides goods and services pursuant to various legal authorities that allow agencies to place orders with another agency. OPM provides background investigation services to over 100 executive branch agencies; however, others, including some agencies in the Intelligence Community, have been delegated authority from the

Office of the Director of National Intelligence, OPM, or both, to conduct their own background investigations.[14]

The National Defense Authorization Act for Fiscal Year 2004[15] permitted the transfer of the federal government's personnel security clearance investigation function from DOD's Defense Security Services to OPM's Federal Investigative Services. In February 2005, DOD transferred its personnel security investigations function and about 1,800 investigative positions, and made a onetime fund transfer of $49.4 million to OPM. The conditions of the transfer were specified in the 2004 Memorandum of Agreement, which detailed the financial and personnel transactions between the two agencies.[16] Since the transfer, DOD relies upon OPM for nearly all of its clearance investigations outside the Intelligence Community.

OPM manages intragovernmental funds transfers from requesting agencies using a revolving fund, which finances a cycle of business-type operations. OPM's revolving fund, authorized under section 1304 of Title 5 of the United States Code, charges executive branch agencies for the sale of background investigation-related products and services when the investigation is scheduled by the requesting agency, and uses the

---

[14]In 2005, the Office of Management and Budget designated OPM as the agency responsible for, among other things, the day-to-day supervision and monitoring of security clearance investigations, and for tracking the results of individual agency-performed adjudications, subject to certain exceptions. However, the Office of the Director for National Intelligence can designate other agencies as "authorized investigative agenc[ies]" pursuant to 50 U.S.C. 435b(b)(3), as implemented through Executive Order 13467. Alternatively, under 5 U.S.C.1104(a)(2), OPM can redelegate any of its investigative functions subject to performance standards and a system of oversight prescribed by OPM under 5 U.S.C. 1104(b). Agencies that have delegated authority from the Director of National Intelligence include, but are not limited to, the Defense Intelligence Agency, National Security Agency, National Geospatial-Intelligence Agency, Central Intelligence Agency, Federal Bureau of Investigation, National Reconnaissance Office, and Department of State. Agencies that have delegated authority from OPM are the Department of Homeland Security (Headquarters, Immigration and Customs Enforcement, Customs and Border Protection, U.S. Secret Service, and U.S. Coast Guard), Bureau of Alcohol, Tobacco and Firearms and Explosives, Bureau of Engraving and Printing, Bureau of the Public Debt, U.S. Agency for International Development, Broadcasting Board of Governors, Department of State, and the Millennium Challenge Corporation.

[15]Pub. L. No. 108-136, § 906 (2003).

[16]Department of Defense and Office of Personnel Management, *Memorandum of Agreement Concerning the Transfer of Certain Elements of the U.S. Department of Defense to the U.S. Office of Personnel Management* (October 2004).

proceeds to finance its costs, usually on a self-sustaining basis.[17] OPM provides its customer agencies with an annual background investigation product pricing list for the upcoming fiscal year in August or September, and bills monthly according to the rate in effect at the time the customer agency places an order for an investigation.

OPM provides a variety of investigative services depending upon the needs of the client agency and the suitability or security clearance requirements of an applicant's position. For example, if an agency requires a secret clearance, OPM would schedule an appropriate level investigation and conduct a series of record checks to determine the applicants' eligibility for a secret clearance.

Many background investigation types have similar components. For all investigations, information that applicants provide on electronic applications are checked against numerous databases.[18] Many investigation types contain credit and criminal history checks, while top secret investigations also contain citizenship, public record, and spouse checks as well as reference interviews and an Enhanced Subject Interview to gain insight into an applicant's character. Although it is not standard, the Enhanced Subject Interview can also be triggered for lower-level investigations if an investigation contains issues that need to be resolved in accordance with the Federal Investigative Standards. Table 1 highlights the investigative components generally associated with the suitability, secret, and top secret clearance levels.

---

[17]Although revolving funds are generally self-sustaining, some, including OPM's, are permitted to carry surplus funds from year to year. Additionally, because revolving funds amount to a permanent authorization for a program to be financed, in whole or in part, through the use of its collections to carry out future operations, they serve as a form of permanent appropriation.

[18]The electronic applications for all investigation types are collectively known as the electronic Questionnaires for Investigations Processing (e-QIP).

**Table 1: Information Gathered in Conducting a Typical Investigation to Determine Suitability and Eligibility for a Security Clearance**

| Type of information gathered by component | Type of background investigation | | |
|---|---|---|---|
| | Suitability | Secret | Top Secret |
| **1. Personnel security questionnaire:** The reported answers on an electronic SF-85P or SF-86 form | X | X | X |
| **2. Fingerprints:** Fingerprints submitted electronically or manually | X | X | X |
| **3. National agency check:** Data from Federal Bureau of Investigation, military records, and other agencies as required | X | X | X |
| **4. Credit check:** Data from credit bureaus where the subject lived/worked/attended school for at least 6 months | X | X | X |
| **5. Local agency checks:** Data from law enforcement agencies where the subject lived/worked/attended school during the past 10 years or—in the case of reinvestigations—since the last security clearance investigation | V | X | X |
| **6. Date and place of birth:** Corroboration of information supplied on the personnel security questionnaire | | | X |
| **7. Citizenship:** For individuals born outside of the United States, verification of U.S. citizenship directly from the appropriate registration authority | | | X |
| **8. Education:** Verification of most recent or significant claimed attendance, degree, or diploma | V | V | X |
| **9. Employment:** Review of employment records and interviews with workplace references, such as supervisors and coworkers | V | V | X |
| **10. References:** Data from interviews with subject-identified and investigator-developed leads | V | V | X |
| **11. National agency check for spouse or cohabitant:** National agency check without fingerprint | | | X |
| **12. Former spouse:** Data from interview(s) conducted with spouse(s) divorced within the last 10 years or since the last investigation or reinvestigation | | | X |
| **13. Neighborhoods:** Interviews with neighbors and verification of residence through records check | V | V | X |
| **14. Public records:** Verification of issues, such as bankruptcy, divorce, and criminal and civil court cases | | | X |
| **15. Enhanced Subject Interview:** Collection of relevant data, resolution of significant issues or inconsistencies | a | a | X |

Source: DOD and OPM.

Note: The content and amount of information collected as part of a personnel security clearance investigation is dependent on a variety of case-specific factors, including the history of the applicant; however, items 1-15 are typically collected for the types of investigations indicated.

V = Components with this notation are checked through a mail voucher sent by OPM's Federal Investigative Services.

[a]The Enhanced Subject Interview was developed by the Joint Reform Team and implemented by OPM in 2011 and serves as an in-depth discussion between the interviewer and the subject to ensure a full understanding of the applicant's information, potential issues, and mitigating factors. It is included in a Minimum Background Investigation, one type of suitability investigation, and can be triggered by the presence of issues in a secret level investigation.

OPM's Federal Investigative Services employs both federal and contract investigators to conduct work required to complete background investigations. The federal staff constitutes about 25 percent of Federal Investigative Services' investigator workforce, while OPM currently also has firm fixed price contracts for investigative fieldwork, among other services, with three contract investigation firms, constituting the other 75 percent of its investigator workforce. According to OPM officials, the prices that the private firms charge OPM for each type of investigation are fixed by OPM's contracts with those firms, and the competition between firms helps keep prices down. Further, OPM officials stated that the mix of federal and contract workforce allows them to respond to the changing investigative demands of the executive branch.

In contracting for investigative fieldwork, OPM typically uses indefinite-delivery, indefinite-quantity contracts that provide for a variety of investigative field work and support services at a fixed price.[19] When OPM selects contractors for its overarching indefinite delivery, indefinite-quantity contract, officials stated that they assess the proposals for both technical and price considerations. While technical expertise is the primary factor in awarding the contract, all else being equal, OPM will select based on the best value, according to OPM documents. OPM officials explained that when assessing the prices of proposals for work, they consider not just the lowest price and the reasonableness of the prices for each case type, but also the contractor's experience and the type of work the contractor wishes to perform.

As the government's primary background investigation provider and the Suitability Executive Agent of the Performance Accountability Council, OPM has been involved in the governmentwide effort to improve and align the background investigations process across the federal government. Over the past several years, the Performance Accountability Council, through the Joint Reform Team at the working level, has evaluated the efficiency of the security clearance process, including technologies for increased automation, to further reduce impediments to

---

[19]Indefinite-delivery, indefinite-quantity contracts allow the government to buy goods and services within the stated limits when the exact times and exact quantities of future deliveries of goods and services are not known at the time of award. The government places orders for individual requirements during the term of the contracts. FAR §§ 16.501-2 and 16.504. According to OPM officials, OPM's indefinite-delivery, indefinite-quantity contracts for investigative fieldwork are fixed price contracts, meaning that prices cannot change as a result of the actual costs incurred by the contractor in performing the work.

the timeliness of investigations, while at the same time minimizing the resources required. Numerous congressional oversight hearings and legislative reforms, such as the Intelligence Reform and Terrorism Prevention Act of 2004 and the Intelligence Authorization Act for Fiscal Year 2010, along with the committed leadership of the Performance Accountability Council, have greatly contributed to the progress of the governmentwide reform.[20]

The Performance Accountability Council also has provided input into revising the Federal Investigative Standards that govern the investigative process to improve the quality of investigations and minimize duplication to allow an investigation to be reciprocally accepted from one agency to another. As part of the revision of the standards, the Joint Reform Team is currently in the process of developing a tiered investigative model.[21] This tiered model is envisioned to reduce the number of investigation types and will align investigations for national security and public trust positions to a greater degree.

## OPM Reported Costs Have Continually Increased While Workload Has Declined in Recent Years

OPM's reported cost data suggest that the overall costs incurred by OPM's Federal Investigative Services to conduct background investigations for the majority of the executive branch have increased by about 79 percent since fiscal year 2005, even though OPM workload has declined since fiscal year 2008. Specifically, OPM's reported costs increased from about $602 million in fiscal year 2005 to almost $1.1 billion in fiscal year 2011, more than a 10 percent average annual increase in fiscal year 2011 constant dollars.[22] OPM's workload experienced a steady increase between fiscal years 2005 and 2008, peaked at approximately 1.7 million stand-alone investigations in fiscal year 2008, and then declined to approximately 1.2 million background

---

[20]Pub. L. No. 108-458, § 3001 (2004) and Pub. L. No. 111-259, § 367 (2010).

[21]The Joint Reform Team proposed a three-tiered model in 2008, but the team continues to refine the model because agencies had concerns, including those of a legal nature, that it did not meet both suitability and security needs, as intended.

[22]These costs include Intelligence Community employee background investigations that OPM conducts.

investigations in fiscal years 2010 and 2011.[23] Figure 2 shows OPM's reported costs by expense type for fiscal years 2005 through 2011. In order to show real growth and compare Federal Investigative Services costs since fiscal year 2005, we adjusted for inflation by converting those costs to constant fiscal year 2011 dollars. For a description of OPM's costs in nominal, or current year dollars, see appendix II. In addition, we relied on OPM's reported cost data for the purposes of our report; however, the extent to which these data are reliable is unknown because an audit of OPM's revolving fund has not been conducted. Further, independent audits of OPM's overall financial management system, where revolving fund transactions are recorded, conducted during fiscal years 2005 through 2011 found material weaknesses in internal controls[24] that could affect the reliability of the cost data cited in this report.

[23]OPM currently offers 13 stand-alone investigative products. We define stand-alone investigations as those that result in suitability determinations, top secret or secret clearances. Other investigations are add-on items that would not by themselves support a suitability or security clearance determination, such as national credit checks or Federal Bureau of Investigation name checks.

[24]Sections 3515 and 3521 of Title 31 of the United States Code require, among other things, that covered agencies like OPM prepare annual audited financial statements covering all accounts and associated activities of each office, bureau, and activity of that agency. OPM's financial statements must be audited either by its Inspector General or an independent external auditor. OPM's financial audits for fiscal years 2005-2011 were conducted by independent audit authority KPMG.

**Figure 2: Federal Investigative Services Reported Costs (In Fiscal Year 2011 Dollars) and Stand-Alone Investigation Workload for Fiscal Years 2005 through 2011**

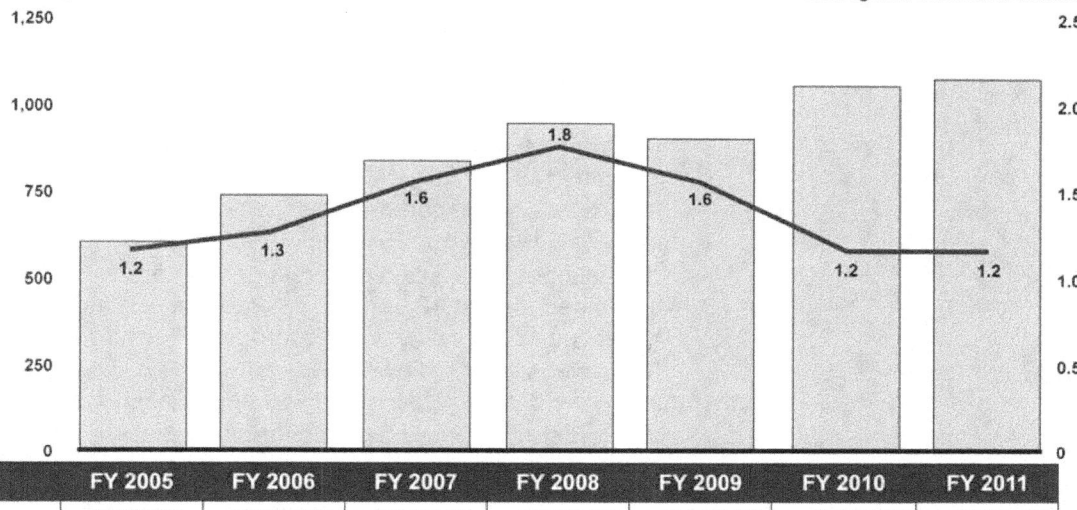

| | FY 2005 | FY 2006 | FY 2007 | FY 2008 | FY 2009 | FY 2010 | FY 2011 |
|---|---|---|---|---|---|---|---|
| Pay and benefits/personnel | 105,582,673 | 182,563,257 | 209,703,474 | 224,196,310 | 213,123,246 | 222,202,823 | 265,373,471 |
| Rent, communication, technology | 13,859,100 | 11,917,328 | 16,211,732 | 15,493,870 | 14,963,382 | 15,223,099 | 17,602,411 |
| Information technology | 11,666,104 | 14,858,541 | 14,478,468 | 40,672,551 | 41,106,908 | 59,327,751 | 91,286,610 |
| End-to-end contract | 355,780,852 | 333,600,552 | 66,897,955 | 13,669,403 | 5,195,563 | — | — |
| Fieldwork contracts | 19,432,261 | 92,080,329 | 345,700,646 | 474,373,580 | 437,034,430 | 485,607,290 | 476,036,406 |
| Support contract | — | 510,640 | 60,756,155 | 56,994,728 | 58,257,059 | 57,300,278 | 55,576,837 |
| Other services | 96,074,320 | 101,931,926 | 124,724,515 | 122,180,422 | 134,702,382 | 217,352,180 | 170,917,677 |
| **Total costs** | **$602,395,310** | **$737,462,573** | **$838,472,944** | **$947,580,864** | **$904,382,970** | **$1,057,013,421** | **$1,076,793,412** |

—— Number of investigations (workload)

▢ Total OPM costs in fiscal year 2011 dollars

Source: GAO analysis of OPM data.

Note: The extent to which these cost data are reliable is unknown because independent audits found material weaknesses in internal controls for OPM's overall financial management system that generated these cost data. Cost categories are defined below.

Pay and benefits/personnel: Salaries and benefits paid to Federal Investigative Services' federal employees.

Rent, Communication and Technology: Rent paid to the General Services Administration, commercial payments, and expenses for wireless phone services, Internet service providers, and mail.

Information technology: Includes information technology rental agreements, the operation and maintenance of hardware and software, and specialized technical services related to upgrading Federal Investigative Services' core suite of technologies.

End-to-end contract: Investigative services provided by contractors, replaced by separate fieldwork and support contracts and phased out from fiscal years 2005 through 2009.

Fieldwork contracts: Fieldwork investigative services provided by contractors that conduct background investigations.

Support contract: Investigation support and mail services provided by contractors, such as data entry and verification.

Other services: Includes travel, training for federal investigators, fees for third-party checks, payments to OPM Common Services, operations and maintenance of facilities, and equipment.

FY = fiscal year

According to OPM officials, the three principal cost factors driving OPM's program are (1) contractor personnel, (2) federal personnel, and (3) investments in information technology.[25] The first cost driver is investigation fieldwork and support contracts, which represent nearly half of OPM's fiscal year 2011 reported costs—about $532 million.[26] Overall, data suggest that costs of investigation fieldwork and support contracts increased almost 42 percent between fiscal years 2005 through 2011 (in fiscal year 2011 dollars).[27] According to OPM officials, the investigative fieldwork contract allows OPM to assign an investigation to a contractor and have it completed for a fixed price.[28] According to OPM officials, the support contract buys clerical support for case-management, including receiving and scheduling investigations as well as scanning necessary documents into the investigative file.[29] The second cost driver is personnel compensation and benefits for OPM's background investigation federal workforce, which represent about 25 percent of OPM's fiscal year 2011 reported costs—about $265 million. OPM's data suggest that personnel compensation increased by 151 percent between fiscal years 2005 through 2011. Federal investigators constitute about 25 percent of OPM's total investigator workforce. In fiscal year 2011, OPM's Federal Investigative Service employed 2,656 individuals, of which 1,581 were

---

[25] We define cost drivers as factors that influence or contr bute to the expense of business operations, and in this case the operation is OPM Federal Investigative Services' background investigations program.

[26] The figure of $532 million was calculated by adding fiscal year 2011 costs for Fieldwork Contracts ($476 million) and Support Contracts (almost $56 million) in fig. 2.

[27] To calculate the increase in costs of OPM contracts during the period of our review, we calculated the increase in total contract costs, including end-to-end contracts, fieldwork contracts, and support contracts.

[28] Each investigation type has a unique price. However, the contractor cannot charge more than what is agreed upon for the type of investigation. For example, if a secret investigation results in more interviews and in-person checks than a typical investigation, the contractor may still only charge the fixed price agreed upon.

[29] According to OPM officials, contractor support functions include receiving the case, data entry, verification, delivery, and administrative support, among other things.

federal investigators who are primarily responsible for high-profile and specialized cases, such as conducting investigations for contractor investigators and political appointees. The third cost driver is OPM's information technology investments. While these investments represent less than 10 percent of fiscal year 2011 reported costs, they have increased more than 682 percent over 6 years (in fiscal year 2011 dollars), from about $12 million in fiscal year 2005 to over $91 million in fiscal year 2011. Further, according to OPM officials, some costs for information technology are also included in other categories, such as rent, communication, technology, and other services. Between fiscal years 2005 and 2007, these costs were primarily for the operation and maintenance of OPM's information technology for processing background investigations, while after fiscal year 2008, information technology costs increased as a result of Federal Investigative Services' modernization effort, known as EPIC modernization, according to officials.[30]

In addition to the three cost drivers, OPM officials identified other changes that were increasing the program's costs. Specifically, officials cited changes to the investigative standards, the 2011 addition of the more-comprehensive Enhanced Subject Interview, increased Federal Bureau of Investigation (FBI) fingerprint and name search fees, and compliance with mandated timeliness requirements as additional factors affecting the cost of investigations. Although the Enhanced Subject Interview requires more labor hours than the previous subject interview, officials from OPM customer agencies stated that the Enhanced Subject Interview, which has an associated, one-time charge of $550, replaced a similar OPM investigation product, the Special Interview, which cost customer agencies $480 each time an investigator made contact with an applicant. In addition, the FBI fee increase from fiscal year 2010 to fiscal year 2011 was $3 per investigation, which affected OPM's operating costs. According to GAO calculations, this increase totals approximately $6.9 million, or less than 1 percent of OPM's total costs, if each investigation in OPM's fiscal year 2011 overall workload includes an FBI fee. Further, as Federal Investigative Services has expanded over the years since it acquired DOD's background investigation program, its common services payments (e.g., from the Federal Investigative Services revolving fund to

---

[30]EPIC is a suite of eight automated background investigation processing tools used by OPM to modernize and streamline the investigation process. The EPIC suite includes, among other systems, an electronic background information questionnaire, an electronic imaging system, an electronic case processing system, and a centralized background investigation verification system.

OPM for the use of OPM-wide support resources) have increased. These services include security, the information technology helpdesk, legal assistance, congressional and legislative affairs, and the Chief Financial Office and internal oversight.

Despite the consistent increase in costs, Federal Investigative Services' workload for stand-alone investigations ultimately declined, after it peaked in fiscal year 2008, as reflected in table 2 below. Over the past several years, the number of stand-alone cases for all major investigation types (top secret, secret, and suitability) has markedly decreased. Specifically, OPM's workload for stand-alone investigations decreased by almost 31 percent since 2008, and its total workload for all investigation types decreased by almost 7 percent since 2008. Further, the number of secret cases handled by Federal Investigative Services declined in fiscal year 2011 by almost 20 percent of the fiscal year 2008 caseload, and suitability, by about 48 percent of the 2008 caseload.

**Table 2: OPM's Federal Investigative Services Workload, Fiscal Years 2005-2011**

| Investigation type[a] | | Fiscal years | | | | | | |
|---|---|---|---|---|---|---|---|---|
| | | 2005 | 2006 | 2007 | 2008 | 2009 | 2010 | 2011 |
| Stand-alone investigations | Top secret | 145,427 | 168,387 | 230,422 | 241,103 | 202,786 | 199,444 | 225,168 |
| | Secret | 529,096 | 609,218 | 710,234 | 714,360 | 595,983 | 553,411 | 575,614 |
| | Suitability | 467,462 | 528,906 | 681,875 | 773,805 | 749,042 | 403,698 | 400,586 |
| | Other | 15,112 | 18,772 | 21,473 | 22,439 | 22,193 | 21,710 | 20,068 |
| | **Total stand-alone investigations** | **1,157,097** | **1,325,283** | **1,644,004** | **1,751,707** | **1,570,004** | **1,178,263** | **1,221,436** |
| Add-on investigation products | Special Agreement Checks | 321,584 | 431,511 | 546,616 | 581,845 | 535,095 | 891,378 | 939,700 |
| | Special Interviews (SPIN) / Enhanced Subject Interviews | 64,768 | 85,810 | 131,058 | 143,564 | 131,806 | 130,075 | 143,473[b] |
| | **Total add-on investigation products** | **386,352** | **517,321** | **677,674** | **725,409** | **666,901** | **1,021,453** | **1,083,173** |
| **Total investigation workload** | | **1,543,449** | **1,842,604** | **2,321,678** | **2,477,116** | **2,236,905** | **2,199,716** | **2,304,609** |

Source: GAO analysis of OPM data.

Notes: OPM does not define or categorize its products with stand-alone or add-on designations, as we did for purposes of this report.

[a]For purposes of this table, OPM investigation case types have been consolidated into either suitability or the clearance level that they support. In addition, initial investigations and reinvestigations have been consolidated.

[b]Enhanced Subject Interviews replaced SPINs in fiscal year 2011 and therefore 143,473 represents the number of Enhanced Subject Interviews for that fiscal year.

In addition to these stand-alone investigations, OPM has other investigative products that contribute to its workload and affect OPM's costs, which we refer to as add-on investigations for the purposes of this report and which are also listed in table 2. Special Agreement Checks are investigation components, such as fingerprint checks or credit checks, that provide additional coverage to a background investigation and are either triggered by information present in the investigation or ordered by the customer agency requesting the background investigation to aid in prescreening an applicant. Special Agreement Checks range in price from $4 to $69, and, according to OPM officials, the number of these record checks almost tripled from fiscal year 2005 through fiscal year 2011 because they (1) replaced other OPM products that were discontinued and (2) included electronic fingerprints, versus mailed.

## OPM Focuses on Recovering Full Operating Costs When Determining Prices, and Does Not Provide Its Customer Agencies Transparent Information on Price Increases

OPM develops prices for its various types of background investigations by using an average cost pricing model focused on full cost recovery, which is intended to recover all Federal Investigative Services' operating costs for each fiscal year. While OPM provides its customers and the public with general information on reasons for price increases, OPM has not been sufficiently transparent with cost details to help customer agencies better understand background investigation price increases.

### Federal Investigative Services' Pricing Model Is to Fully Recover Operating Costs

Since 1952, OPM (or its predecessor agency, the Civil Service Commission) has financed elements of its background investigations program through a revolving fund, which means that revenues recovered from customer agencies ( i.e., prices for background investigations products) pay for the program's fiscal year operating costs (including both the costs of conducting an investigation and overhead costs).[31] According to Federal Investigative Services officials, they use an average cost model to help ensure that their prices set for each new fiscal year will

---

[31]GAO, *OPM's Revolving Fund Policy Should Be Clarified and Management Controls Strengthened*, GGD-84-23 (Washington, D.C.: October 1983).

cover the overall costs they will incur for providing background investigations that fiscal year. We have previously reported that fees set at an average rate may be higher or lower than the actual costs of providing services to specific users.[32]

Each year, Federal Investigative Services officials estimate their total costs and calculate the total anticipated revenue for the coming year. To develop the prices of its investigation products, OPM estimates revenue for the upcoming year, which is based upon OPM's expected investigation workload, multiplied by the current prices, adjusted to cover projected costs for the coming fiscal year. As a result, prices are set to fully recover operating costs, and, in some cases, have led to a surplus for OPM such as in fiscal year 2007 through fiscal year 2010 as demonstrated in table 3. To develop prices, OPM officials described a three-step process, as shown in figure 3. This mechanism has not essentially changed in the past two decades although OPM's overall workload has substantially increased between fiscal years 2005 through 2008 as a result of the 2005 transfer of DOD's investigative function to Federal Investigative Services, which is reflected in table 2.

---

[32]GAO, *Federal User Fees: A Design Guide,* GAO-08-386SP (Washington, D.C.: May 29, 2008).

**Figure 3: OPM's Calculation of Final Prices for Its Various Investigation Types**

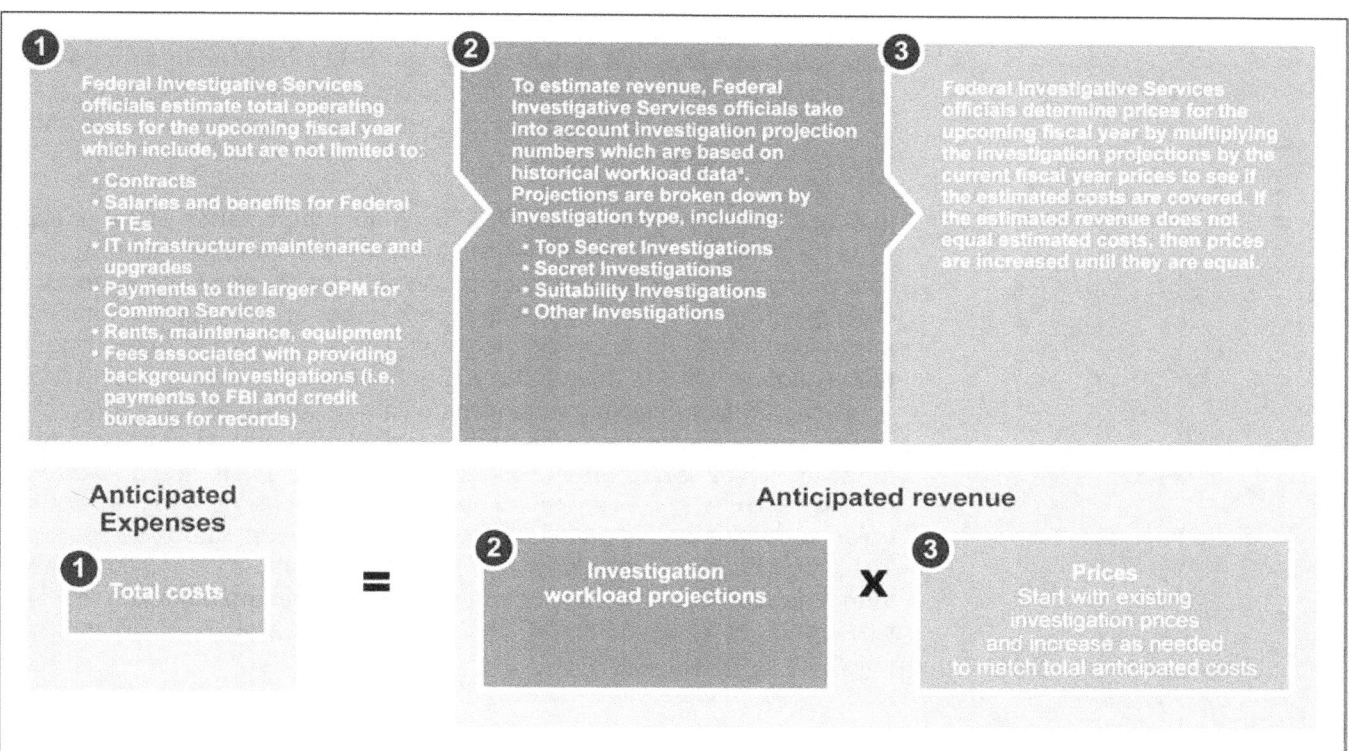

Source: GAO analysis of OPM data

[a]Customer agencies are asked to provide workload projections that are accurate within a 5 percent margin to assist OPM in estimating costs for the upcoming year. However, OPM officials stated that, due to the unreliability of agency projections, OPM instead uses agency investigation workloads from the previous fiscal year to project numbers and types of background investigations.

The first step in setting prices, according to OPM officials, is to estimate costs and assess the balance of the revolving fund to determine the remaining cost to be covered by the revenue from investigations in the coming fiscal year. To estimate its costs for the coming year, OPM projects its operating expenses in accordance with major budget object class categories outlined in Office of Management and Budget Circular No. A-11, such as personnel compensation and benefits, contractual services and supplies, payments for contractors and General Services

Administration rent, and acquisition of assets like equipment.[33] OPM's reported information about costs—such as investigative contractor fieldwork and support costs, and internal investments associated with conducting investigative services such as OPM's planned information technology investments from fiscal year 2008 through 2014 to modernize its systems—is gathered from various points of contact within OPM and Federal Investigative Services.

In addition to estimating costs, OPM considers the balance or net position of its revolving fund. Federal Investigative Services finances its costs by collecting revenue from customer agencies (fees for providing services to other agencies) through a revolving fund, rather than through annual appropriations. GAO has previously noted that, while OPM's revolving fund is not required to operate on a break-even basis over the short term, operating OPM's revolving fund with deficits or surpluses for 5 or more years is not consistent with the statutory goal of operating each activity on an actual cost basis to the maximum extent feasible.[34] In response, OPM adopted 3 years to 5 years as an appropriate time frame within which to balance surpluses and deficits. However, in fiscal years 2007 through 2010, OPM's revolving fund, as a whole, had a surplus, or more revenue than it needed to cover costs, each year. The total surplus during the 5-year period of fiscal years 2007 through 2011 was over $227 million, as indicated in table 3 below.

[33]Section 83 of Office of Management and Budget Circular No. A-11 breaks down budget object class categories and codes to be used in presenting obligations by the items or services purchased by the federal government.

[34]GAO, *OPM Revolving Fund: Investigation Activities During Fiscal Years 1983 Through 1986,* GGD-87-81 (Washington, D.C.: June 26, 1987) and GAO, *OPM Revolving Fund: OPM Sets New Tuition Pricing Policy,* GGD-94-120 (Washington, D.C.: Apr. 6, 1994). Section 1304 of Title 5 of the United States Code states that to the maximum extent feasible, OPM shall conduct each individual activity financed by the revolving fund on an actual cost basis over a reasonable period of time.

**Table 3: Federal Investigative Services' Costs, Revenue, and Differences for Fiscal Years 2007 to 2011, in Nominal Dollars**

| | Fiscal years | | | | | |
|---|---|---|---|---|---|---|
| | 2007 | 2008 | 2009 | 2010 | 2011 | Total |
| Revenue | $838,427,517 | $1,034,737,301 | $929,143,514 | $1,063,298,353 | $1,063,298,207 | **$4,928,904,892** |
| Total costs | 788,541,880 | 911,828,638 | 882,831,524 | 1,041,390,763 | 1,076,793,412 | **4,701,386,217** |
| Difference between costs and revenue[a] | 49,885,637 | 122,908,663 | 46,311,990 | 21,907,590 | (13,495,205) | **227,518,675** |

Source: GAO analysis of OPM data.

Note: This analysis of Federal Investigative Services data is in nominal dollars to reflect actual financial position for the time period. We do not show fiscal years 2005 and 2006 revenue because the funds transferred from DOD to OPM during that time period, as indicated in the Memorandum of Agreement between the agencies, prevented a simple accounting of revenue.

[a]Difference values may vary due to rounding.

Further, according to Federal Investigative Services officials, OPM's goal is to maintain a net position, or balance within a 5 percent margin of its revenue,[35] which they maintained, on average, during the fiscal years 2007 through 2011. In addition, agency officials stated that the net position or balance allows flexibility for OPM to incur losses in some years and have surpluses that make up for the losses in other years to break even as described above. Also, OPM maintains retained earnings that would be sufficient to close out its operations through leases, contracts, and other items, and officials said that from fiscal years 2008 through 2010 the agency used the balance of the revolving fund minus the retained close out costs to fund information technology projects, such as EPIC modernization.

After costs are estimated and the net position of the revolving fund considered, OPM then estimates the investigation workload for the next fiscal year. The workload projections are broken down by investigation type because each of OPM's investigative products has different components and therefore contractors charge OPM different prices for each investigation type. To estimate workload, officials stated that they primarily rely on historical trends for each agency's workload. In addition,

---

[35]OPM strives to maintain a 5 percent net margin, but there is some variance from year to year depending on how much OPM relies on the revolving fund balance to invest in information technology upgrades. For example, the percentage of the surplus ranged from -1 percent to 12 percent, with an average of 5 percent.

GAO-12-197 Background Investigations

OPM also considers workload projections provided by customer agencies for the upcoming fiscal year.

Lastly, OPM uses the prices of its products in the current fiscal year as a starting point and adjusts them accordingly to help ensure projected costs are covered in the coming year, which may result in increasing prices when necessary. Once prices have been estimated, OPM compares the change in price, if any, to changes in the Consumer Price Index–All Urban Consumers.[36] Additionally, OPM has an established review process for both its case pricing procedure and the prices themselves. Both the Associate Director of Federal Investigative Services and the Chief Financial Officer of OPM approve prices, and brief the Director of OPM on price changes for the upcoming year when requested.

## OPM Does Not Provide Stakeholders with Transparent Cost Data Used to Determine Prices

Although OPM reports on its prices before the start of each fiscal year, agencies do not have access to detailed information about how prices are linked to costs, and therefore some customer agency officials have stated that they do not understand the basis for OPM's prices and price increases over time. Some agencies that use OPM background investigation services, such as DOD, have asked for more detailed cost data in support of OPM's increase in prices. However, OPM does not provide an explanation or crosswalk that links its costs to the prices charged for the services because (1) its prices include costs other than those associated with specific investigative component costs, such as overhead for fees provided to OPM for common services like information technology help desks, and (2) it aggregates all overhead costs. OPM's prices are a projection of what it expects to spend in the next fiscal year. We have previously identified key operating principles to guide the management of revolving funds, and among those principles is the need for a transparent and equitable pricing methodology that allows agencies

---

[37]The Consumer Price Index for All Urban Consumers is a measure of the average change over time in the prices paid by urban consumers for a market basket of consumer goods and services.

to recover total costs.[37] Further, if customers understand how a rate is determined and changed, including the assumptions used by the agency setting the rate, those customers can anticipate potential changes and incorporate that information into their budget plans. In addition, according to *Federal User Fees: A Design Guide*, providing program information to other agencies, stakeholders, and Congress, can improve transparency, ensure that prices remain aligned with program costs and activities, and increase awareness of the costs of the federal program,[38] such as OPM's Federal Investigative Services. While OPM's pricing methodology is designed to recover its costs, OPM does not provide this cost information to agencies. Instead, OPM provides a list of billing rates for the coming fiscal year, without supporting information and other guidance, through memos called Federal Investigations Notices, published annually in August or September. The notices are sent to agencies through OPM liaisons and are also publicly available on the Federal Investigative Services website.

According to DOD officials, one of the reasons that OPM's investigation prices are not transparent is that the final amount that customer agencies pay for stand-alone investigations is often higher than the prices OPM advertises for such investigations in its Federal Investigations Notices. Federal Investigations Notices publish prices for stand-alone investigations that, by themselves, would support a suitability determination, or secret or top secret clearance. The notices also contain prices for investigation products that are additional to stand-alone investigations. These add-ons, such as an Enhanced Subject Interview, are triggered by applicant circumstances found in the investigation, such as extensive international travel, a poor credit report, or record of illegal

---

[37]GAO, *Intragovernmental Revolving Funds: Commerce Departmental and Census Working Capital Funds Should Better Reflect Key Operating Principles*, GAO-12-56 (Washington, D.C.: Nov. 18, 2011). GAO identified four key operating principles to guide the management of intragovernmental revolving funds, such as that used by OPM to finance its background investigations, including (1) clearly delineating roles and responsibilities, (2) ensuring self sufficiency by recovering the agency's total costs, (3) measuring performance, and (4) building in flexibility to obtain customer input and meet customer needs.

[38]GAO-08-386SP. GAO developed *Federal User Fees: A Design Guide,* which examines the characteristics of user fees, and factors that contribute to a well-designed fee. While fees paid to OPM for clearance investigations are not traditional user fees, which are fees assessed to private users for goods or services provided by the federal government, several aspects of the *Federal Design Guide* can serve as good practices to consider when managing interagency fees.

conduct, all of which would require further investigation. DOD officials stated that the prices contained in OPM's Federal Investigative Notices are not always reflective of the amount DOD actually pays for an investigation, as a result of these add-on investigations. For example, in fiscal year 2011, OPM's published price for a military servicemember's secret[39] clearance investigation was $228, but the actual average price that DOD ultimately paid for this type of investigation was $350 as a result of add-ons, according to DOD calculations. Further, OPM's published price for a civilian's secret[40] clearance investigation in fiscal year 2011 was $260, while, according to DOD, the average price DOD paid for this type of investigation was $427. As a result, DOD's fiscal year 2011 requests for these two types of clearances cost about $65 million more than the published price in OPM's Federal Investigation Notices.

Excluding add-on investigation products, our trend analysis showed that the percentage change in stand-alone investigation prices generally exceeded selected measures of inflation, even though OPM considers one of those measures, the Consumer Price Index–All Urban Consumers, in its price calculations. Overall, the prices of OPM stand-alone investigation types experienced an average annual percent increase of 3.1 percent to 7.9 percent over the period of fiscal years 2005 through 2012, although OPM did not increase any investigation prices in fiscal years 2010 and 2012. As a specific example, the investigation that supports a military servicemember's secret clearance increased in price from $160 in fiscal year 2005 to $228 in fiscal year 2012, presenting an average annual price increase of 5.5 percent, compared to the average annual Consumer Price Index–All Urban Consumers increase of 2.6 percent. See appendix III for the prices and percentage change in prices for all OPM investigative products from fiscal years 2005 through 2012, and our analysis comparing weighted average annual percentage change in prices to changes in selected measures of inflation, including the

[39]The type of investigation used in this example is a National Agency Check with Law and Credit, and this price is based on OPM's fiscal year 2011 Federal Investigations Notice.

[40]The type of investigation used in this example is an Access National Agency Check with Inquiries, and this price is based on OPM's fiscal year 2011 Federal Investigations Notice.

Consumer Price Index–All Urban Consumers and the Employment Cost Index.[41]

According to Federal Investigations Notices, the reason OPM did not increase investigation prices in fiscal years 2010 and 2012 was because Federal Investigative Services was able to absorb increases in operating costs, which means that the balance in the revolving fund was more than the amount OPM needed to fund operations and maintain to close out operations, if needed. Further, OPM officials said they believe it is OPM's responsibility to pass on cost savings to customers whenever it is able to do so, including by keeping prices at current levels in fiscal years 2010 and 2012. However, some officials from OPM customer agencies said they did not understand why the prices of lower-level suitability investigations had continued to increase most years between fiscal years 2005 and 2011 despite few, if any, changes having been made to process requirements for these investigations. Based on the information provided in the notices and on testimonial evidence, OPM presents only very broad reasons for price increases and has never provided customer agencies with detailed explanations of why it needs to increase prices in most years, but not in some others. As a result, agency officials expressed dissatisfaction with OPM's price increases.

OPM does not determine the prices of its investigations by assessing the costs of the components that make up investigations, such as those components listed in table 1, because according to OPM officials, it is time-intensive and inefficient to determine the exact cost of each individual investigation. Further, officials said that each type of background investigation contains different requirements, and investigations that have the same requirements will still contain varying components, which are driven by the background of the individual applicant who is being investigated. For example, investigations cover a specified time period and are composed of a number of leads based on the applicant's credit, public records, law checks, references, employment, residences, and education, among other things. As the number of these elements contained in an investigation increases, so does the amount of labor required to complete it. While this is the case for

---

[41] In using a weighted average approach to calculate the average, a category that has a greater proportion of items would receive a greater weight in calculating the average. The Employment Cost Index is a quarterly measure of changes in labor costs. We used the Employment Cost Index for total compensation for all civilian workers.

OPM's federal workforce conducting investigations, OPM contractors charge a fixed price for each investigation type that it completes (which represents about 75 percent of the investigations completed). We also found that the Joint Reform Team attempted to document cost information by each investigative component to inform the team's decisions about potential changes to the investigative process. However, according to Reform Team officials and senior OPM officials, they were unable to document total cost by investigative components, such as neighborhood checks and subject interviews. Officials from the Joint Reform Team said that although they were able to determine actual cost by investigation component, they were not able to break down the cost of OPM's overhead by component because OPM does not have the details of the overhead cost data that would be required to do this. We also requested these data and OPM officials said it was not available because they use an average cost model.

Nonetheless, the perceived lack of transparency regarding OPM's prices creates customer agency dissatisfaction when they compare OPM's prices with those of contractors. For example, several agencies we spoke to noted that individual contracting firms' prices were much lower than OPM's prices and felt that OPM included excessive overhead in its prices. For example, officials from customer agencies that have delegated authority to conduct their own investigations noted that they directly contract with private investigation providers whose prices for a top secret investigation were as much as $1,500 lower than OPM's prices. However, some customer agencies noted that OPM has additional costs as a centralized investigative provider that needed to be covered by its pricing.

In response to this lack of transparency surrounding OPM's pricing, some agency officials said they believe they can obtain background investigative services that are cheaper than OPM's rates and are considering other options, such as using or seeking delegated authority from the Director of National Intelligence to perform their own background investigations and planning to hire private investigation firms to perform the work. For example, officials at the Department of Homeland Security recently told us they considered exercising delegated authority to conduct the agency's own investigations. According to officials, its Personnel Security Division considered using delegated authority that the department already had, instead of voluntarily using OPM to conduct their investigations, because of cost and time considerations including that there is a significantly lower cost for top secret investigations when dealing directly with the contractors. However, OPM is the primary service provider for most executive branch agencies that require background investigations.[42] The risk of agency distrust of OPM's prices may be reduced if OPM clearly reports its methods for price setting, including an accounting of operating costs and the assumptions used to project future program costs and revenue. Transparent processes for reviewing and updating fees help assure payers and other stakeholders that fees are set fairly and accurately and are spent on the programs and activities intended. If more agencies move toward obtaining delegated authority, duplication in technology and processes may result, which would dilute any cost efficiencies that could be gained by having investigative services centrally conducted. In addition, reciprocity may be affected if multiple agencies are conducting their own background investigations. For example, when not conducted centrally, each background investigation may be subject to varying criteria for completeness and quality, such as more stringent suitability requirements. Further, the application of the revised federal investigative standards across the government could be hindered by agencies' differing processes and application of those standards for investigations. Ultimately, agencies may become reluctant to reciprocally accept a suitability determination or security clearance because of these potential inconsistencies.

Although customer agencies lack clarity over OPM background investigation prices, we noted that some communication between OPM and customer agencies on the prices of investigations does occur. For example, the Background Investigation Stakeholders Group is a group of agency policy representatives that meet on a monthly basis. This forum provides an opportunity for OPM to communicate with its customer agencies. OPM stated that it shares draft Federal Investigations Notices at these meetings. In addition, a number of agencies, including the Department of Homeland Security and the Department of Justice, hold interagency agreements with OPM, which serve as an official record of the amounts transferred between the agencies for investigative services, and some, though not all, agencies consider them useful when developing their budgets. Although, according to OPM officials, it may not be efficient to identify the specific costs per investigation or how to distribute overhead costs to each investigation, OPM has opportunities for providing customer agencies with more information supporting its price

---

[42]While OPM was designated as the agency responsible for the day-to-day supervision and monitoring of security clearance investigations, and for tracking the results of individual agency-performed adjudications, some executive branch agencies have delegated authority to conduct their own investigations. These agencies with delegated authority are primarily within the Intelligence Community.

changes. For example, information about Federal Investigative Services' principal cost factors driving the aggregated operating costs, including contracts, federal personnel costs, and information technology investments, would improve customers' understanding of how OPM determined or changed investigation prices. However, OPM does not share information with its customers annually in its Federal Investigations Notices about its operating costs, which are the basis for investigation prices. Some customer agency officials stated that in the absence of a cost-based explanation for OPM price increases over the years, they did not have a context to assess the value of changes to investigative processes. Such information would help customer agencies better understand the reasons for investigation price changes, and as a result, customers would be better positioned to anticipate potential changes to those assumptions, identify their effect on costs, and incorporate that information into their budget planning.

## The Governmentwide Suitability and Personnel Security Clearance Reform Efforts Have Not Yet Focused on Cost Savings

Governmentwide reform efforts have yet to address or focus upon cost efficiencies and savings related to the investigation process, although these reform efforts resulted in increased coordination and cooperation to help improve investigation and adjudication timeliness challenges. Both the Intelligence Reform and Terrorism Prevention Act (IRTPA) of 2004 and the resulting reform effort's strategic framework[43] established objectives for timeliness and quality. Additionally, the strategic framework also included cost efficiency as part of its mission statement. The Performance Accountability Council—with the Joint Reform Team at the working level—as leaders of the governmentwide reform effort, have not focused on identifying and eliminating process inefficiencies within OPM's portion of the investigation process. The Performance Accountability Council is positioned to further improve upon the previous successes of reform by focusing future efforts on identifying cost-savings opportunities in the background investigation process. For example, Executive Order 13467 makes the Performance Accountability Council responsible for ensuring and overseeing the development of tools and techniques for enhancing background investigations and the making of eligibility determinations.

---

[43]Performance Accountability Council, *Security and Suitability Process Reform Strategic Framework* (Washington, D.C.: February 2010). This report was created under the Performance Accountability Council by the Joint Reform Team.

In previously issued reports, we noted the need for the reform effort to address costs and pursue cost savings in the background investigation process. In 2008 we testified that the Joint Reform Team should ensure that Congress is provided with the long-term funding requirements necessary to implement any proposed changes to the current clearance processes.[44] Such requirements would enable the executive branch to compare and prioritize alternative proposals for reforming the clearance processes, especially as the nation's fiscal imbalances constrain federal funding. Further, we recommended in May 2009 that members of the Joint Reform Team specify the funding and budget requirements for reform-related efforts, and estimate any potential cost savings that could result from reform.[45] To date, members of the Joint Reform Team have not taken steps to provide Congress with this information, which is especially critical in the current fiscal environment and may hinder oversight functions related to the governmentwide background investigation reform effort. Despite our previous calls for a focus on costs, we noted that no documented cost savings are currently being pursued by leaders of the reform effort. Further, OPM officials explained that some of the reform-related requirements, such as the required completion time for investigations, may increase OPM operating costs, which could lead to increases in investigation prices. However, during the course of this review, we identified two areas of potential duplication and inefficiency that suggest opportunities exist to improve upon the current investigation processes and if successfully addressed, could generate cost savings.

---

[44]GAO, *Personnel Clearances: Key Factors to Consider in Efforts to Reform Security Clearance Processes*, GAO-08-352T (Washington, D.C.: Feb. 27, 2008).

[45]GAO, *Personnel Security Clearances: An Outcome-Focused Strategy Is Needed to Guide Implementation of the Reformed Clearance Process*, GAO-09-488 (Washington, D.C.: May 19, 2009).

## Agencies Have Made Duplicative Investments in Case-management and Adjudication Systems

We found that multiple agencies have invested or plan to individually invest in case-management and adjudication systems to meet their specific needs.[46] In an effort to better manage the adjudication portion of the suitability and security clearance process, agencies have transitioned or planned to transition from a paper-based to an electronic adjudication case-management system. Although the investment in electronic case-management systems will likely lead to process efficiencies, agencies may not be leveraging adjudication technologies in place at other executive branch agencies to minimize duplication.

According to DOD officials, DOD began the development of its Case Adjudication Tracking System in 2006 and has invested a total of $32 million since then to deploy the system. The system helped DOD achieve efficiencies with case-management and an electronic adjudication module for secret level cases that did not contain issues, given the volume and types of adjudications performed. After observing that the Case Adjudication Tracking System could easily be deployed to other agencies at a low cost, DOD officials said that the department intended to share the technology with interested entities across the federal government. The Department of Energy is piloting the electronic adjudication module of DOD's system and, according to DOD officials, the Social Security Administration is also considering adopting the system. In addition to DOD, Department of Justice officials said they began developing a similar system in 2007 at a cost of approximately $15 million.

Five other agencies are also developing or seeking funds to develop systems with similar capabilities as shown in table 4. With multiple agencies developing individual case-management systems, these agencies may be at risk of duplicating efforts and may fail to realize cost savings. DOD officials suggested that opportunities may exist to leverage their case-management technology. However, DOD officials explained that agencies would have to initially invest approximately $300,000 for implementation, plus any needed expenditures related to customizations,

---

[46]The adjudication phase of the suitability determination or security clearance processes occurs at the agency requesting a background investigation, and is separate from the investigation that OPM conducts. Adjudicators from the requesting agency use the information from the investigative report to determine whether an applicant is eligible for a security clearance. To make suitability and clearance eligibility decisions, federal requirements specify that adjudicators consider guidelines in 13 specific areas that elicit information about (1) conduct that could raise security concerns and (2) factors that could allay those security concerns and permit granting a clearance.

and long-term support and maintenance, which could require approximately $100,000 per year.

**Table 4: Adjudication System Investments**

| Agency | Purpose | Development stage | Investment |
|---|---|---|---|
| Department of Defense (DOD) | Case-management, electronic adjudication, adjudication record repository | Developed and implemented across most of DOD services | $32 million |
| Department of Homeland Security | Adjudication record repository | Developed and implemented | $6.5 million[a] |
| Department of the Treasury | Case-management | In-progress, seeking funds | $300,000[b] |
| Office of Personnel Management (OPM) | Case-management and electronic adjudication | Initiated with Request for Information | To be determined |
| Department of Justice | Case-management and electronic adjudication | In-progress | $15 million[c] |
| Department of Veterans Affairs | Case-management and electronic processing | Under development by a private contractor | $900,000 |
| National Reconnaissance Office | Case-management and electronic adjudication | Under development in-house | $6.8 million |

Source: GAO.

[a]This figure represents the amount that the Department of Homeland Security spent to consolidate several adjudication systems within the department over the past 5-year period and is inclusive of software license fees, enhancements, interfaces, and data-migration development and support. The current system, the Integrated Security Management System, supports approximately 1300 users at seven DHS components. These costs are offset by the retirement of six legacy case-management systems and their associated support costs.

[b]According to Treasury officials, this figure represents the estimated sought amount for development and implementation of a Department of the Treasury case-management and adjudication system.

[c]This figure represents Department of Justice's Justice Security Tracking Adjudication Record System-related investments since 2007.

In addition to DOD and other agency efforts, OPM officials explained that they also plan to develop an electronic case-management system for purchase by customer agencies that is synchronized with its governmentwide background investigations system. OPM put out a request for information to evaluate the options for this system. DOD responded to OPM's request for information by performing a comparative analysis of its own case-management system and said that it believes its system meets the needs set out in OPM's request for information. However, OPM officials said that DOD's system would cost too much money for smaller agencies to adopt, so OPM plans to continue exploring other options that would allow customer agencies access to their electronic case-management system without the need to make an expensive initial investment. Additionally, OPM officials said that their effort is intended to promote process efficiency by further integrating OPM with its more than 100 customer agencies. However, some OPM customer agencies including DOD, which makes up approximately 75 percent of OPM's investigation workload, expressed concern that such a system would likely be redundant to currently available case-management technology. Further, any overhead costs related to the development of an OPM system would be incorporated into OPM's operating costs, which could affect investigation prices.

Although the investment in electronic case-management systems aligns with the reform effort's goal to automate information technology capabilities to improve the timeliness, efficiency, and quality of existing security clearance and suitability determinations systems and will likely lead to process efficiencies, agencies may be unclear how they might achieve cost savings through leveraging adjudication technologies in place at other executive branch agencies. In its March 2009 Enterprise Information Technology Strategy, the Joint Reform Team stated that agencies will leverage existing systems to reduce duplication and enhance reciprocity.[47] Further, Executive Order 13467, states that the Performance Accountability Council is responsible for ensuring and overseeing the development of tools and techniques for enhancing background investigations and the making of eligibility determinations, such as adjudication of security clearances, and for establishing requirements for enterprise information technology. As such, it is positioned to promote coordination and standardization related to the suitability and security clearance process through issuing guidance to the agencies. While the reform effort's strategic framework includes cost savings in its mission statement, this framework lacks specificity regarding how agencies might achieve costs savings. Without specific guidance, the opportunities to minimize duplication and achieve cost savings may be lost.

---

[47] Joint Security and Suitability Reform Team, *Enterprise Information Technology Strategy* (Washington, D.C.: Mar. 17, 2009).

## OPM Has Not Studied Cost Savings Opportunities within Its Own Background Investigations Process

OPM is planning an assessment of its background investigation process; however, the study is limited to OPM's workforce and will not include an assessment of work processes. During the course of our review we identified a number of process inefficiencies. OPM's background investigation process is complex, as shown in figure 4, which provides a general summary of the process's key steps.

**Figure 4: Key Steps in OPM's Background Investigation Process**

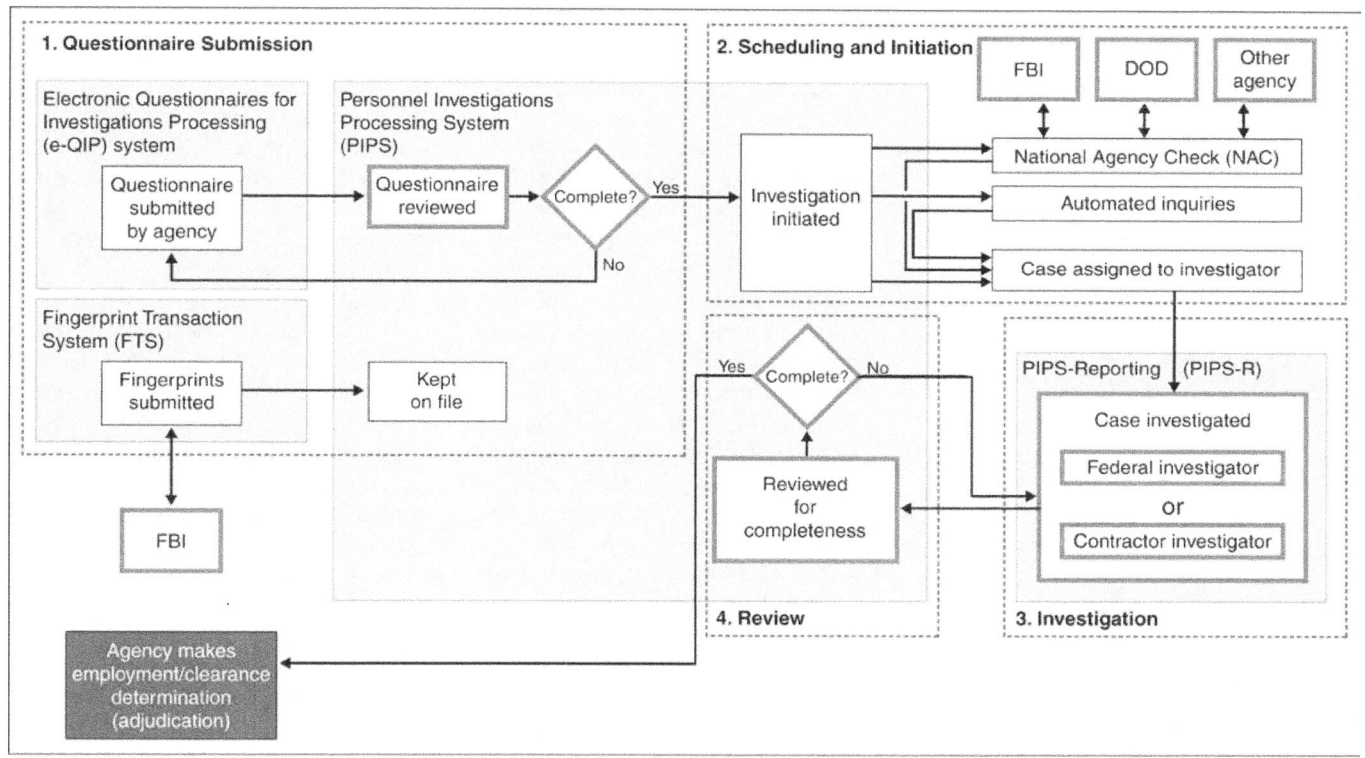

Human interaction

Automated process

Source: GAO analysis of OPM data.

Although this figure generally summarizes OPM's background investigation process, it does not account for the range and number of investigative components, collected in steps 2 and 3, because of the complexity and variability inherent to each investigation given the circumstances of the applicant.

OPM officials explained that, to date, they have chosen to address investigation timeliness and investigation backlogs rather than the identification of process and workforce efficiencies. To its credit, OPM helped reduce the backlog of ongoing background investigations that it inherited from DOD at the time of the 2005 transfer. Additionally, OPM has taken initial steps to begin addressing quality challenges. However, only recently has OPM started to look at its internal processes for efficiencies. While OPM seeks to identify optimal staffing levels, as mentioned before, the request for information excludes the identification of possible process efficiencies, which could lead to cost savings. The following are examples of potential cost-savings opportunities we observed during the course of this review:

- *OPM's Double Charge (with Reimbursement) for Fingerprints Causes Extra Labor:* According to OPM officials, OPM workload has tripled for fiscal years 2005 through 2011; however, OPM overall workload may be inflated because some Special Agreement Checks, one type of OPM add-on investigation, are charged twice. For example, according to DOD and Department of Homeland Security officials, OPM counts some add-on investigations, specifically fingerprints, more than once, even though the fingerprints pertain to the same investigation request. Fingerprinting precedes the scheduling of the investigation and is also included as part of the package for investigations in support of secret and top secret clearances. Not only does this practice inflate OPM's workload, but it also affects OPM and its customer agencies, in several ways. First, OPM needs to refund its customer agencies for its initial charge. For example, DOD is charged $24.25 for an individual's fingerprint, then $4,005 for a top secret clearance investigation, which also includes $24.25 for an electronic fingerprint. As a result, OPM's reimbursement represents additional labor associated with OPM's clearance process. Second, customer agencies are burdened by the need to track the reimbursements from OPM to ensure that refunds are received and to reconcile OPM's workload numbers with their own, to eliminate the double counting.

- *OPM's investigation process reverts its electronically-based investigations back into paper-based files:* In November 2010, the Deputy Director for Management of the Office of Management and Budget testified that OPM now receives 98 percent of investigation applications electronically, yet we observed that it is continuing to use a paper-based investigation processing system and convert electronically submitted applications to paper. OPM officials stated that the paperbased process is required because a small portion of their customer agencies do not have electronic capabilities. However,

OPM's process has not been studied to identify efficiencies. As a result, OPM may be simultaneously investing in process streamlining technology while maintaining a less efficient and duplicative paper-based process.

While the primary focus of the governmentwide reform effort has been on improving timeliness and quality of investigations and adjudications, given the pressure government agencies are under to reduce costs there may be opportunities for governmentwide cost savings. Specifically, the Performance Accountability Council is well-positioned to identify opportunities for cost-savings within the process, such as duplications of resources across multiple agencies for case-management and adjudication systems. Further, OPM—as both a member of the Performance Accountability Council and the provider of investigative services for the majority of the executive branch outside of the Intelligence Community—has an opportunity to identify efficiencies within its overall investigation process that could result in cost savings and, ultimately, lower prices for agencies governmentwide.

## Conclusions

OPM is responsible for conducting millions of background investigations that determine individuals' suitability for public trust positions, clear individuals for access to sensitive or classified information, and reevaluate these credentials on a periodic basis. Because OPM charges its customer agencies fees for providing these investigations, transparency over how its costs align with the prices charged and, in particular, how changes in price reflect changes in costs, are key to building successful working relationships. Especially in the current fiscal environment as federal agencies are trying to identify areas where costs can be reduced, it is essential that agencies understand the composition of the costs that constitute the prices of their investigations. While we recognize some of the challenges OPM faces in disaggregating its costs to more directly link its costs to its prices, a more transparent rate-setting process would help assure that customers are being charged accurately and fairly for services supported through OPM's revolving fund. Moreover, transparent cost information, which forms the basis of OPM background investigation prices, could facilitate stronger and more successful working relationships with customer agencies and help with congressional oversight of the suitability and security clearance processes. Further, detailed and accurate information on OPM's costs to conduct background investigations can help inform the decisions of officials from agencies that are considering seeking authority to conduct their own investigations as a potential way of saving money.

In addition to transparency of costs, the Performance Accountability Council, through the Joint Reform Team, is working to reform the overall security clearance process as part of an interagency effort. As part of this effort early on, officials described balancing cost efficiency, improved timeliness, and high-quality products. Given the attention to timeliness, and to some extent quality, and the current pressures on federal agencies to reduce costs of operations, the Performance Accountability Council and OPM have an opportunity to focus on process efficiencies that could lead to cost savings. Any efficiencies gained have the potential to affect agencies across the federal government. Further, since the Performance Accountability Council represents many federal agencies, its position provides an opportunity to facilitate governmentwide coordination that could prevent duplication of effort and result in cost savings.

## Recommendations for Executive Action

To improve transparency of costs and the efficiency of suitability and personnel security clearance background investigation processes that could lead to cost savings, we recommend that

- the Director of OPM direct the Associate Director of Federal Investigative Services
  - to provide customer agencies with better information on the costs of background investigations, including the data related to its main cost drivers in order to clarify, to the extent possible, how its costs align with and affect investigation prices; and
  - to take actions to identify process efficiencies that could lead to cost savings within its background investigation process; and that

- the Deputy Director for Management, Office of Management and Budget, in the capacity as Chair of the Performance Accountability Council, expand and specify reform-related guidance to help ensure that reform stakeholders identify opportunities for cost savings, such as preventing duplication in the development of electronic case-management and adjudication technologies in the suitability determination and personnel security clearance processes.

## Agency Comments and Our Evaluation

In commenting on a draft of our report, the Office of Management and Budget and OPM concurred with our recommendations directed toward those agencies. Additionally, DOD provided us comments noting that the observations and recommendations described in the report provide sound justifications for pursuing greater efficiencies and cost savings. We received oral comments from the Office of Management and Budget, and those comments are summarized below. OPM and DOD's written comments are reprinted in their entirety in appendixes IV and V, respectively. OPM and DOD also provided us with technical comments, which we incorporated in this report, as appropriate.

In oral comments, the Office of Management and Budget concurred with our recommendation that the Deputy Director for Management, in the capacity as Chair of the Performance Accountability Council, help its reform partners identify continued administrative efficiencies and opportunities for cost savings. In addition, the Office of Management and Budget agreed that OPM should improve the information it provides customer agencies about the drivers of its operating costs and investigation prices. The Office of Management and Budget noted it appreciated that this report assessed the cost of background investigations with respect to the larger scope of the ongoing governmentwide suitability and security clearance reform efforts. Further, OMB provided additional comments that we took into consideration.

- First, Office of Management and Budget officials encouraged us to review the context of our presentation of OPM's workload, particularly our analysis of stand-alone investigations. We reviewed our presentation of OPM's workload data, and believe that our interpretation of that information is correct. In deciding to separate the workload, we primarily considered that some of the customer agencies expressed concerns that OPM's overall workload may be inflated because some Special Agreement Checks, one type of OPM add-on investigation, are charged twice, as described on page 34 of our report. Finally, in response to Office of Management and Budget comments about our workload presentation, we consolidated two tables from our draft report and added a line that displays OPM's total workload, see table 2.
- Second, Office of Management and Budget officials asked us to consider using the same year as the baseline for analysis of changes in investigation workload and costs. We agree, and the scope of our report is fiscal years 2005 through 2011, as stated in appendix I. In response to OMB's comment, we also compared the changes in workload and costs from fiscal years 2008 through 2011. Our analysis of OPM workload data indicates that, regardless of the fiscal year used as a baseline, OPM workload is decreasing. Specifically we found that OPM's costs increased by almost 14 percent in fiscal year 2011 dollars between fiscal years 2008 and 2011, while OPM's workload for stand-alone investigations decreased by almost 31 percent, and its total workload for all investigation types decreased by 7 percent.

- Lastly, the Office of Management and Budget encouraged us to consider addressing why OPM's investigation prices may be perceived as more expensive than those investigations acquired through direct authority with a private contractor, and the nonmonetary costs and benefits of using such contracts. We did not address why OPM's background investigation prices may be perceived as more expensive than those acquired through a private contractor or the costs and benefits of OPM versus private investigative service providers because that analysis is outside the scope of this report and would require additional work. However, we noted that some agencies that we met with felt OPM's overhead was justified as a governmentwide central investigative provider.

In written comments, OPM concurred with our recommendation to provide customer agencies with better information on the costs of background investigations. Specifically, OPM agreed that its background investigations stakeholders require transparency from Federal Investigative Services in order to anticipate and plan for cost changes in background investigations and described an initial action it took to improve transparency. In addition, OPM concurred with our recommendation to take actions to identify business process efficiencies. OPM noted that these actions also reinforce a Federal Investigative Services priority and that the agency will continue to map its processes to achieve maximum process efficiencies and identify potential cost savings. While concurring with our recommendation, OPM stated that it did not agree with our basis for reaching it. Specifically, OPM identified some areas of concern in our report as addressed below.

- *Cost drivers:* OPM did not agree with our characterization of its cost drivers for the Federal Investigative Services background investigation program on page 14 of this report. Specifically, in its agency comments, OPM expressed the view that we misrepresented primary operational costs as cost drivers and then cited the Federal Accounting Standards Advisory Board's definition of a cost driver, which defines a cost driver as "any factor that causes a change in the cost of an activity or an output." We disagree because, while we recognize the advisory board's definition, we identified the cost drivers on the basis of the available documentation of OPM's costs. Therefore, for purposes of this report, we define cost drivers as a factor that influences or contributes to the expense of business operations, and in this case the operation is OPM Federal Investigative Services background investigations program. To identify Federal Investigative Services cost drivers, we analyzed cost data provided by Federal Investigative Services and identified its largest operating costs. Further, our report cites other factors in addition to the three cost drivers that OPM officials said affected their operating costs, including more-comprehensive subject interviews, increased FBI fees, and compliance with investigation timeliness requirements, as discussed on page 15. While we recognize that the additional drivers identified by OPM in its comments on a draft of this report—congressionally mandated timeliness requirements, elimination of investigation backlog, workload shifts toward more costly investigations, and delivery of suitability and security processes—may affect their total operating costs, OPM does not capture cost information in a way that allows it to document those costs as drivers. Further, OPM did not provide documentation to support how the additional drivers that officials identified affected costs or cite the amount that costs increased as a result of those drivers.

- *Information technology spending:* In its comments, OPM stated that we made no attempt to benchmark Federal Investigative Services information technology costs, and provided technical corrections about our characterization of its information technology investment category of costs, which we applied to the report. We disagree that we did not benchmark information technology costs. As stated in the report, the total growth of information technology costs between fiscal years 2005 and 2011 is 682 percent, and the average annual growth rate is 40.9 percent. We acknowledge that information technology cost increases are the result of EPIC modernization by stating on page 15 that, according to OPM officials, information technology costs were primarily for EPIC modernization. In addition, we focused on actual costs incurred to date on information technology, which we cite as being driven by EPIC, through fiscal year 2011. Further, although OPM officials updated us on the status of EPIC modernization, they did not provide documentation of EPIC modernization cost estimates through 2014.

- *Strategic goals of reform:* OPM stated in its comments that we mischaracterized the goals of the governmentwide suitability and security clearance reform effort. In our draft report, we stated that cost savings is a goal of the reform effort. We have modified this report to reflect that the overall mission statement of the governmentwide suitability and security clearance strategic framework includes timeliness and quality, as well as cost efficiency. Therefore we believe that the reform effort's strategic goals—timeliness, quality, reciprocity, an integrated database, end-to-end information technology automation, suitability and security alignment, and continuous evaluation—should be implemented with the mission of cost efficiency in mind. Further, in a previous GAO report in which we recommended that the reform effort develop its mission statement and strategic goals, DOD and Office of the Director for National Intelligence officials cited that the aims of reform were to achieve comprehensive reform of the end-to-end security clearance process delivering high-assurance security clearances fairly, efficiently, and at the lowest reasonable cost to the federal government.

- *Workload and cost data:* OPM's said we inaccurately applied OPM-provided workload and cost data. We disagree that our application of the data was inaccurate; however, in response, we added the total workload numbers that OPM provided for this report in table 2. We also acknowledge that OPM does not define or categorize its products with stand-alone or add-on designations, as we did for purposes of this report. As stated above in our response to input from the Office of Management and Budget, we separated the workload as a result of customer agency concerns that OPM overall workload may be inflated. For example, some Special Agreement Checks, one type of OPM add-on investigation, are charged twice. In addition, our analysis indicates that OPM's total workload has declined 7 percent since it peaked in fiscal year 2008.

- *Data reliability:* OPM stated that we inaccurately characterized the facts of the audit of OPM's revolving fund and that the findings of the financial audits that we reviewed do not impact the reliability of the data provided for this report. We disagree. It is GAO policy and a requirement of the Government Auditing Standards to assess the reliability of all data used in the report. As OPM acknowledged during the course of our work, an audit of OPM's revolving fund has not been conducted. Therefore, we concluded that the reliability of the cost data provided by Federal Investigative Services is unknown. In addition, independent audits of OPM's overall financial management system, now the Consolidated Business Information System, conducted during fiscal years 2005 through 2011 found that there were material weaknesses or significant deficiencies in internal controls related to the information control environment. Because there were problems with internal controls at the consolidated level—the level on which the audits were conducted—we concluded that it was possible that problems also exist at the Federal Investigative Services level, which was not audited. Therefore, given weaknesses and deficiencies in internal controls at the consolidated level and that the revolving fund has not been audited, the extent to which the financial data are reliable is unknown.

We addressed other specific OPM comments at the end of appendix IV.

In written comments, DOD stated that the observations and recommendations contained in our report provide sound justification for the further pursuit of cost efficiencies. In addition, DOD stated that it questions 1) the basis of OPM's background investigation prices, 2) OPM's information technology investments, and 3) OPM's investigation billing processes. Finally, DOD noted that reciprocity should not be affected by the use of multiple investigative service providers. We did not include in our scope the use of multiple investigative service providers.

As agreed with your offices, unless you publicly announce the contents of this report earlier, we plan no further distribution until 30 days from the report date. At that time, we will send copies to the Office of Management and Budget, OPM, and DOD. In addition, the report will be available at no charge on the GAO Web site at http://www.gao.gov.

If you or your staff have any questions about this report, please contact me at (202) 512-3604 or farrellb@gao.gov. Contact points for our Offices of Congressional Relations and Public Affairs may be found on the last page of this report. GAO staff who made major contributions to this report are listed in appendix VI.

Sincerely yours,
Brenda S. Farrell
Director, Defense Capabilities and Management

# Appendix I: Scope and Methodology

This report reviewed the Office of Personnel Management's (OPM) Federal Investigative Services' pricing model for all investigation products, including both suitability and personnel security clearance background investigations. In addition, we examined OPM's relationship with its customer agencies and OPM's role in the governmentwide reform effort. We relied on OPM's reported cost data for the purposes of our report; however, the extent to which these data are reliable is unknown because an audit of OPM's revolving fund[1] has not been conducted. Independent audits found material weaknesses in internal controls for OPM's overall financial management system, where revolving fund transactions are recorded, and these weaknesses could affect the reliability of the cost data contained in this report. Those audits, which are mandated by sections 3515 and 3521 of Title 31 of the United States Code and executed annually by KPMG, also made recommendations to OPM to correct the material weaknesses. Nonetheless, these are the only cost data available and what OPM uses to develop background investigation prices.

To identify cost trends related to OPM's background investigations since 2005 and determine the principal factors that drive OPM costs, we obtained and analyzed relevant documentation from key OPM representatives, listed in table 5.

---

[1]An intragovernmental revolving fund is an appropriation account authorized to be credited with collections from other federal agencies' accounts that are earmarked to finance a continuing cycle of business-type operations. According to the Office of Management and Budget, collections of intragovernmental revolving fund accounts are derived primarily from within the government. GAO, *A Glossary of Terms Used in the Federal Budget Process*, GAO-05-734SP. (Washington, D.C.: September 2005). The self-sustaining nature of these accounts means that funds received in exchange for services remains available for authorized purposes without needing to be reappropriated, subject to certain conditions.

**Table 5: Office of Personnel Management (OPM) Offices Interviewed**

| Federal Investigative Services | • Associate Director |
| | • Billing Oversight |
| | • Business Management |
| | • Customer Services |
| | • Field Management |
| | • Management Services and Oversight |
| | • Processes and Systems Modernization |
| Chief Financial Office | |
| Special Advisor to the Director of OPM | |

Source: GAO.

Through interviews with knowledgeable OPM officials from Federal Investigative Services and the Chief Financial Office, we obtained and reviewed Federal Investigative Services' expenditures from fiscal years 2005 through 2011, and converted those data to fiscal year 2011 dollars in order to assess real growth and account for inflation. Further, we obtained documentation of Federal Investigative Services' workload by investigation type for fiscal years 2005 through 2011 in order to describe the workload trends and compare them to cost trends for the same period. To assess the reliability of these workload data maintained within OPM's Personnel Investigations Processing System, we reviewed and updated our 2010 data reliability assessments by discussing reliability-related issues with OPM officials. We found these workload data sufficiently reliable for our purposes.

To assess how OPM develops the background investigation prices charged to agencies and the extent to which the basis of these prices is transparent, we interviewed the offices listed in table 6, including the Department of Defense (DOD)—OPM's largest customer—and five additional executive branch agencies that use OPM to conduct background investigations for their employees. We selected these executive branch agencies in table 6 on the basis of their ability to meet a combination of one or more of the following criteria: (1) utilizes OPM to conduct most of its security clearance investigations for civilians, military, and industrial (contractor) personnel; (2) ranks among OPM's top ten largest investigation customers, by volume and/or by total expenditures in fiscal year 2010; and (3) is a member of the Performance Accountability Council. Because this is a nonprobability sample, our findings do not generalize to the agencies that we did not include in our review.

**Table 6: Executive Branch Customer Agencies Interviewed**

| Executive branch agency | Associated departments and offices |
|---|---|
| Department of Defense (DOD) | • The Office of the Under Secretary of Defense for Intelligence<br>• Defense Security Services<br>• Defense Personnel Security Research Center<br>• Defense Business Transformation Agency<br>• DOD Intelligence Community agencies;<br>    • Defense Intelligence Agency<br>    • National Security Agency<br>    • National Reconnaissance Office |
| Department of Energy | Office of Departmental Personnel Security |
| Department of Homeland Security | Personnel Security Division |
| Department of Justice | Security and Emergency Planning Staff |
| Department of the Treasury | Office of Security Programs |
| Department of Veterans Affairs | Office of Operations, Security, and Preparedness |

Source: GAO.

In addition, we obtained and reviewed (1) OPM's pricing standard operating procedure and related documentation; (2) OPM's annual Federal Investigations Notices that document and publish prices charged to customer agencies for each investigation type; (3) fieldwork and investigation support contracts, (4) the transaction processes between OPM and selected executive branch customer agencies in table 6; and (5) OPM and customer interagency agreements, which serve as an official record of the amounts transferred between the agencies for investigative services. To observe headquarters-level background investigation processes, we conducted a site visit at Federal Investigative Services' headquarters in Boyers, Pennsylvania, and obtained testimonial evidence from knowledgeable officials representing related OPM divisions listed in table 5. These discussions included information on the effect of OPM's process modernization investments and the suitability and personnel security clearance reform effort on prices, and the extent to which OPM discusses price information with its customer agencies. Next, we performed analysis synthesizing documentation of how OPM determines prices on the basis of cost estimations and projections for the upcoming fiscal year with the testimonial evidence we gathered. We also spoke with representatives from three private investigative firms—U.S. Investigative Services, CACI International, and Keypoint Government Solutions—that hold current investigation contracts with OPM to gather general information about how the background investigations conducted for OPM and its customer agencies are assessed for cost and price. However, since contract information is proprietary, we received limited pricing information and did not include it in the report. To understand various perspectives on the extent to which OPM is transparent about its costs and pricing determination with its stakeholders, we met with selected OPM customer agencies in table 6.

To assess the extent to which governmentwide reform efforts have focused on reducing the costs associated with the suitability and personnel security clearance processes, we analyzed various Performance Accountability Council and Joint Reform Team documents, including reform strategic plans. We also reviewed internal OPM reports regarding its background investigation process and information technology initiatives. In addition, we held discussions with knowledgeable officials from the agencies listed above in tables 1 and 2 and met with Joint Reform Team representatives from the Office of the Director for National Intelligence to determine the extent to which (1) relevant background investigation stakeholders have prioritized cost efficiencies within the broader investigation reform effort and (2) agencies have invested resources in modern case-management and adjudication systems. Further, in an effort to understand how OPM officials have sought investigation process efficiencies, we conducted numerous meetings with OPM officials and conducted a site visit at Federal Investigative Services' investigation processing facility in Boyers, Pennsylvania. We also interviewed knowledgeable officials from OPM, DOD, and Office of the Director of National Intelligence to understand the status of reform initiatives and determine the extent to which cost analyses of these initiatives have been conducted.

We conducted this performance audit from March 2011 through February 2012 in accordance with generally accepted government auditing standards. Those standards require that we plan and perform the audit to obtain sufficient, appropriate evidence to provide a reasonable basis for our findings and conclusions based on our audit objectives. We believe that the evidence obtained provides a reasonable basis for our findings and conclusions based on our audit objectives.

# Appendix II: Federal Investigative Services Reported Nominal Costs for Fiscal Years 2005 through 2011

The cost information described in table 7 below was provided for this report by OPM's Federal Investigative Services and corresponds to OPM's reported cost information in figure 2 of this report; however, the reported costs presented in figure 2 have been adjusted for inflation and the reported costs presented below are in nominal, or current year, dollars. Further, the extent to which this cost data is reliable is unknown because independent audits found material weaknesses in internal controls for OPM's overall financial management system that generated this cost data.

**Table 7: Federal Investigative Services Costs (in Nominal Dollars) for Fiscal Years 2005 through 2011**

Nominal dollars

| | Fiscal years | | | | | | |
|---|---|---|---|---|---|---|---|
| | 2005 | 2006 | 2007 | 2008 | 2009 | 2010 | 2011 |
| Pay and benefits/personnel | $93,273,845 | $166,760,581 | $197,215,632 | $215,737,383 | $208,044,519 | $218,918,665 | $265,373,471 |
| Rent, communication, and technology | 12,243,406 | 10,885,764 | 15,246,323 | 14,909,286 | 14,606,805 | 14,998,102 | 17,602,411 |
| Information technology | 10,306,070 | 13,572,386 | 13,616,275 | 39,137,976 | 40,127,330 | 58,450,887 | 91,286,610 |
| End-to-end contract | 314,303,920 | 304,724,088 | 62,914,182 | 13,153,656 | 5,071,753 | | |
| Fieldwork contracts | 17,166,848 | 84,109,856 | 325,114,172 | 456,475,465 | 426,619,900 | 478,430,014 | 476,036,406 |
| Support contract | | 466,439 | 57,138,126 | 54,844,317 | 56,868,793 | 56,453,380 | 55,576,837 |
| Other services | 84,873,976 | 93,108,699 | 117,297,170 | 117,570,555 | 131,492,424 | 214,139,715 | 170,917,677 |
| **Total expenses** | **$532,168,065** | **$673,627,813** | **$788,541,880** | **$911,828,638** | **$882,831,524** | **$1,041,390,763** | **$1,076,793,412** |

Source: OPM

Notes: Cost categories are defined below.

Pay and benefits/personnel: Salaries and benefits paid to Federal Investigative Services' federal employees.

Rent, communication and technology: Rent paid to the General Services Administration, commercial payments, and expenses for wireless phone services, Internet service providers, and mail.

Information technology: Includes information technology rental agreements, the operation and maintenance of hardware and software, and specialized technical services related to upgrading Federal Investigative Services' core suite of technologies.

End-to-end contract: Investigative services provided by contractors, replaced by separate fieldwork and support contracts and phased out from fiscal years 2005 through 2009.

Fieldwork contracts: Fieldwork investigative services provided by contractors that conduct background investigations.

Support contract: Investigation support and mail services provided by contractors, such as data entry and verification.

Other services: Includes travel, training for federal investigators, fees for third-party checks, payments to OPM Common Services, operations and maintenance of facilities, and equipment.

# Appendix III: OPM's Weighted Annual Percentage Change in Prices Is More Than Consumer Price Index and Employment Cost Index for Fiscal Years 2005 through 2012

The Office of Personnel Management (OPM) conducts several different types of investigations. However, three categories of stand-alone investigations (suitability, secret, and top secret) make up approximately half of OPM's workload, but are most labor-intensive. Table 8 below shows that the average annual percent increase in prices for each investigation type ranged from 3.1 percent to 7.9 percent over the period of fiscal year 2005 through fiscal year 2012.

**Table 8: OPM Federal Investigations Notice Investigation Percentage Price Increases by Fiscal Year**

Percent

| Investigation type | | Fiscal years | | | | | | | Average annual percent increase[a] |
|---|---|---|---|---|---|---|---|---|---|
| | | 2005-2006 | 2006-2007 | 2007-2008 | 2008-2009 | 2009-2010 | 2010-2011 | 2011-2012 | |
| Suitability | National Agency Check (NAC) | 5.3% | 3.8% | 15.7% | 6.3% | | 2.9% | | 4.8% |
| | National Agency Check and Inquiries (NACI) | 4.9 | -6.5 | 14.0 | 6.1 | No increase | 3.3 | No increase | 3.1 |
| | Minimum Background Investigation (MBI) | 5.6 | 10.5 | 6.3 | 5.9 | | 27.2 | | 7.9 |
| Secret | National Agency Check with Law and Credit (NACLC) | 25.0 | -4.0 | 9.4 | 5.2 | | 3.2 | | 5.5 |
| | Access National Agency Check and Inquiries (ANACI) | 24.3 | -4.3 | 8.6 | 5.4 | | 3.2 | | 5.3 |
| Top secret | Single Scope Background Investigation (SSBI) | 25.0 | -5.3 | 4.8 | 4.5 | | 3.0 | | 4.6 |
| | Single Scope Background Investigation, Periodic Reinvestigation (SSBI-PR) | 25.2 | -6.3 | 4.9 | 4.6 | | 3.0 | | 4.5 |
| Average of average percent change[b] | | 5.1% | | | | | | | |
| Weighted average percent change[c] | | 20.1% | -4.3% | 10.0% | 5.5% | 0% | 4.6% | 0% | 5.1% |
| Consumer Price Index percent increase[d] | | 3.2 | 4.1 | 2.4 | 5.6 | -2.1 | 1.2 | 3.6 | 2.6 |
| Employment Cost Index percent increase[e] | | 3.0 | 3.4 | 3.0 | 1.9 | 1.8 | 2.2 | - | 2.6 |

Source: GAO analysis of OPM data.

Notes: All price increases are based on standard rates from OPM Federal Investigative Services' annual Federal Investigations Notices. The prices and percent increases provided for 2005 and 2006 reflect the Department of Defense (DOD)-specific rates that OPM charged DOD at that time. After 2007, the DOD premium charge ended and was followed by a rise in prices for all agencies, but DOD's prices decreased slightly.

[a]This column notes the average of the annual percentage price changes for each investigative product from fiscal years 2005 to 2012.

[b]This row presents the simple average of the average annual percent increases.

[c]We calculated weighted percent changes based on the volume of the major case types shown in this table, which represent approximately half of OPM's total caseload in fiscal years 2005 to 2011 for stand-alone investigation types. The weights represent the proportion of total investigations for each investigative type for that year, so investigations representing a larger proportion of the workload received a greater weight. Weights for fiscal year 2012 are not yet available; however, since the price change was zero, the weighted percent change will also be zero.

[d]The CPI percent increases are based on the Consumer Price Index for urban consumers (which measures consumer inflation for all urban or nonfarm consumers) and represent the change from the previous July to the July in which OPM sets prices for the upcoming fiscal year.

[e]The ECI percent increases are based on the Employment Cost Index for total compensation for civilian workers and represent the change from the previous June quarter to the June quarter in which OPM sets prices for the upcoming fiscal year.

We found that the weighted average annual percentage change of prices was 5.1 percent between fiscal years 2005 and 2012. In the weighted average approach, the percentage change in prices for a particular type of investigation is weighted by its share of total investigations. If a category of investigation makes up a larger proportion of total investigations, then its percentage change in prices would receive a greater weight in calculating average annual prices over the period.[1] To calculate the weighted average over the period, we computed the weighted average percentage change in prices for each year. We then averaged these annual averages over the period to get the overall weighted average.

Our trend analysis also showed that OPM prices generally exceed the Consumer Price Index (All Urban Consumers) rate. We found that the weighted average annual percent increase in the investigation prices, 5.1 percent, was about 2.5 percentage points more than the average percent increase in the Consumer Price Index (All Urban Consumers), 2.6 percent. For example, the price of OPM's Minimum Background Investigation (MBI), a type of investigation that supports a suitability determination, increased from $450 in fiscal year 2005 to $752 in fiscal

---

[1]When a simple average is used to calculate an average, each category receives an equal weight in the calculation. In using a weighted average approach in calculating the average, a category that has a greater proportion of items would receive a greater weight in calculating the average. For example, suppose we had two categories of investigations where category A had 90 investigations and category B had 10 investigations, for a total number of investigations of 100. Suppose the percentage change in prices for category A was 3% and for category B it was 5%. If a simple average of percentage change is calculated, the result is 4%. If a weighted average is calculated, the average would be (.9 times 3% plus .1 times 5%) equals 3.2%. This would be a better representation of the overall percentage change in prices.

year 2012, with a 27 percent increase between 2010 and 2011 and an average annual price increase of 7.9 percent, compared to the average annual Consumer Price Index (All Urban Consumers) increase of 2.6 percent. Further, OPM's National Agency Check with Law and Credit (NACLC), a type of investigation that supports a secret clearance, increased in price from $160 in fiscal year 2005 to $228 in fiscal year 2012, presenting an average annual price increase of 5.5 percent, compared to the average annual Consumer Price Index (All Urban Consumers) increase of 2.6 percent. We compared the percent change in investigation prices to percent changes in the Consumer Price Index (All Urban Consumers) because OPM stated it compares its proposed changes in prices to the Consumer Price Index (All Urban Consumers); however, our comparison showed that, overall, OPM price increases were larger than the average annual Consumer Price Index (All Urban Consumers) percentage increase for the respective years.

Further, given that personnel costs make up a large portion of OPM's investigation costs, we compared the weighted average annual percentage change in the prices of investigations to the Employment Cost Index for Total Compensation for civilian workers, which shows the changes in wages, bonuses, and benefits of the nonfarm industries excluding the federal government. As table 8 shows, the average annual percentage change in the Employment Cost Index from 2005 through 2011 was 2.6 percent, while the weighted average annual percentage change in prices over the same period was 5.1 percent. As with the Consumer Price Index (All Urban Consumers), the weighted average annual percentage change in prices of investigations exceeded the percentage change in the Employment Cost Index.

**Table 9: OPM Federal Investigations Notice Prices by Fiscal Year**

Dollars

| | | | | | | Fiscal years | | | | | | |
|---|---|---|---|---|---|---|---|---|---|---|---|---|
| Investigation type | | 2005 | 2005 DOD rate | 2006 | 2006 DOD rate | 2007 | 2008 | 2009 | 2010 | 2011 | 2012 |
| Suitability | National Agency Check (NAC) | $76 | $76 | $80 | $80 | $83 | $96 | $102 | $102 | $105 | $105 |
| | National Agency Check and Inquiries (NACI) | 92 | 102 | 97 | 107 | 100 | 114 | 121 | 121 | 125 | 125 |
| | Minimum Background Investigation (MBI) | 450 | - | 475 | - | 525 | 558 | 591 | 591 | 752 | 752 |
| Secret | National Agency Check with Law and Credit (NACLC) | 125 | 160 | 131 | 200 | 192 | 210 | 221 | 221 | 228 | 228 |
| | Access National Agency Check and Inquiries (ANACI) | 140 | 185 | 147 | 230 | 220 | 239 | 252 | 252 | 260 | 260 |
| Top secret | Single Scope Background Investigation (SSBI) | 3,000 | 3,000 | 3,150 | 3,750 | 3,550 | 3,719 | 3,888 | 3,888 | 4,005 | 4,005 |
| | Single Scope Background Investigation, Periodic Reinvestigation (SSBI-PR) | 1,825 | 2,045 | 2,050 | 2,560 | 2,400 | 2,517 | 2,632 | 2,632 | 2,711 | 2,711 |
| Add-on items | Special Interview (SPIN)[a] | - | 410 | - | 430 | 440 | 460 | 480 | 480 | 550 | 550 |
| | Special Agreement Check (SAC)[b] | 21 | | 22 | | 23 | 24.25 | 24.25 | 24.25 | 24.25 | 24.25 |

Source: GAO analysis of OPM data.

Notes: All prices are based on standard rates from OPM Federal Investigative Services' annual Federal Investigations Notices.

[a]The SPIN was discontinued in 2010 with the Joint Reform Team development of the Enhanced Subject Interview, which replaced the SPIN.

[b]OPM currently offers 17 types of SAC. We used the price of the electronic fingerprint-only SAC.

# Appendix IV: Comments from the Office of Personnel Management

Note: GAO comments supplementing those in the report text appear at the end of this appendix.

UNITED STATES OFFICE OF PERSONNEL MANAGEMENT
Washington, DC 20415

The Director

January 24, 2012

Ms. Brenda S. Farrell
Director, Defense Capabilities Management
Government Accountability Office
441 G St, NW
Washington, DC 20548

Dear Ms. Farrell,

Thank you for the opportunity to respond to GAO's draft report GAO-12-197, "BACKGROUND INVESTIGATIONS: Office of Personnel Management Needs to Improve Transparency of Its Pricing and Seek Cost Savings." Detailed technical comments on the report recommendations are enclosed.

See comment 1.

See comment 2.

Although we agree with GAO's recommendations for improved transparency and process efficiencies, the conclusions drawn from the detailed information OPM provided is often problematic. OPM provided a significant amount of information to support this study, but the report does not always accurately interpret the information or clearly represent the information with appropriate balance. Additionally, we believe that the report provides focus and direction that is inconsistent with many previous GAO recommendations on security clearance processes.

RECOMMENDATION 1: To improve transparency of costs and the efficiency of suitability and personnel security clearance background investigation processes that could lead to cost savings we recommend that:

- The Director of OPM direct the Associate Director of Federal Investigative Services

  o to provide customer agencies with better information on the costs of background investigations, including the data related to its main cost drivers in order to clarify, to the extent possible, how its costs align with and affect investigation prices.
  o to take actions to identify process efficiencies that could lead to cost savings within its background investigation process

OPM RESPONSE:

We concur with the recommendation but not with GAO's basis for reaching the recommendation. Cost transparency is a mission critical business necessity particularly as OPM's Federal Investigative Services (FIS) prepares to implement the Security and Suitability Process Reform's Federal Investigative Standards. As a business operation, we embrace cost

2

transparency in order to succeed in today's fiscal environment. Our stakeholders must be able to better plan and anticipate cost changes and that can only happen if we create greater transparency. The reformed process enhancements and investments are improving the performance and delivered product. Relating the cost benefits to the stakeholders is critical to our reform leadership role.

With regard to GAO's transparency recommendation, OPM FIS has made this a priority and made some progress. Since the spring of 2011, FIS management has focused on creating a process that is more cost-transparent and includes analytical processes that more fully represent and measure costs and performance. With this new infrastructure and data, FIS was able to hold its first "Cost Transparency" briefing with Background Investigations Stakeholders on January 19, 2012. This meeting punctuated a commitment to engage stakeholders in meetings later in the year to give transparency to the pricing FIS develops and to provide stakeholders annual cost and performance reports.

GAO's recommendation to identify process efficiencies also reinforces a FIS priority. Two years ago, OPM FIS began a business process reengineering effort to better position us to adopt new technology and implement reformed Federal Investigative Standards. We will continue to map our processes to achieve maximum process efficiency and identify potential cost savings as we migrate to upcoming standards.

Finally, OPM FIS's commitment to fiscal accountability and cost transparency as an organizational imperative has been specifically communicated to OMB in support of high priority performance goals through 2013.

Although we concur with this recommendation for all of the reasons stated, the basis for the recommendation provided by GAO is unbalanced and skewed negatively. GAO creates many data scenarios to demonstrate cost increases throughout the report but does little to explain the reasons for the increases. This is confusing since the reforms and improvements that explain the costs were all recommended and endorsed by GAO over the years as necessary. By taking this view of program costs, devoid of the context of the major cost drivers that GAO helped create, GAO intentionally leaves information gaps and uses those gaps to support the recommendation that more transparency is needed. Because the first requirement for this audit was "identify the cost trends related to OPM's background investigations and the principal factors *driving OPM costs*," it is not clear why valid cost drivers were left unexplored.

For instance:

- The Federal Accounting Standards Advisory Board's Cost Accounting Dictionary defines "Cost Driver" as any factor that causes a change in the cost of an activity or output"[1]. By failing to accurately represent our four primary cost drivers the report creates an information gap leading to a negative impression of the value of OPM goods and services. The four primary cost drivers are:

---
[1] http://www.fasab.gov/pdffiles/costacc_glossary.pdf

See comments 2, 3, & 4.

3

- congressionally mandated IRTPA timeliness requirements
- elimination of the inherited backlog from DoD
- workload shift towards more costly fieldwork - intensive investigations
- delivery of suitability and security process

- The report misrepresents primary operational costs as "cost drivers," and juxtaposes data in Figure 2 to create the impression that OPM is doing fewer investigations while charging more (charging more for *less*). The report makes no effort to provide balance to that view by accurately representing the information provided by OPM FIS on the cost drivers that explain the figure and demonstrate that costs correlate with investigative activity (charging more for *more*).
- The report fails to give balance by recognizing the incredible improvements to the background investigative program associated with these cost drivers, improvements that were recommended and reinforced in previous GAO reports. We are meeting IRTPA timeliness mandates; we contributed significantly to support DoD's removal from the High Risk List, our timeliness from 145 days in 2005 to 40 days today represents a significant efficiency improvement and has returned billions of dollars of productivity back to the government. These 'efficiency investments' would have provided necessary balance to the primary operational costs on which the report focuses. Previous GAO audits and Congressional testimony provide full evidence of these improvements.
- The report also makes no attempt to benchmark FIS' IT investments against our enterprise and like enterprises to provide context – and to assess true significance. For example, in the report Highlights, GAO states that IT investments "have increased more than 682 percent over 6 years (in FY2011 dollars) from about $12 million in FY 2005 to over $91 million in FY 2011." This is an inaccurate portrayal, since FIS began a significant investment in the modernization of their mission-critical systems (EPIC Transformation) in 2008. From 2005 to 2008 the IT costs were primarily operations and maintenance. The decision by GAO to focus on "percent increase" does not compare apples to apples. If GAO wanted to accurately represent "increase in IT investment costs" it would start with 2008 and would go to projected investments through 2014 to be inclusive of the EPIC modernization (which proceeds while continuing to support 94% of the government's background investigation work). Further, it would provide context to the expenditures by contrasting the expense with similar enterprises (i.e. as a percentage of revenue).
- The report does not accurately represent the strategic reform goals or roles. Reforms strategic goals are clearly stated in the Strategic Framework document recommended by GAO and include:

  - Reciprocity
  - Integrated Database
  - IT Automation
  - Timeliness
  - Security and Suitability Alignment
  - Continuous Evaluation
  - Quality

4

- GAO misrepresents reform goals by stating that "improving cost savings" is a goal, and then indicts the Performance Accountability Council for "not providing executive branch guidance on cost savings." Reform has always focused on large scale savings through IT investments and policy and process streamlining. Despite providing White House documentation to demonstrate OPM's role as a Reform Leader, GAO continues to minimize our role as "involved" vice leading reform.
- The report takes the significant workload and cost data that OPM provided and inaccurately applies it to (Figure 2), attributing certain product types incorrectly to decisions (Table2 and Table 3), inaccurately representing product content (Table 1), and misaligned cost and work data (Table 4).
- Finally, the report inaccurately represents the facts of the audit of OPM's Revolving Fund by associating a "material weakness" to the financial management system that was not portrayed in the audit report and is not in concert with OPM's interpretation of KPMG's audit finding. Per KPMG, the finding was a result of weaknesses in the information system control environment. Specifically, KPMG found security authorization package reviews were not fully effective, monitoring of the security control program could be improved, and implementing new policies to overcome this finding were weak. In OPM's opinion, this finding has no bearing on the quality and reliability of cost data, as GAO implies.

We have worked proudly with GAO over the years to carry the background investigation process to its current healthy state. We have made reform and quality improvements. We have no backlog. We are delivering national security investigations with unprecedented timeliness. This report fails to adequately provide context to FIS operating costs. Impacts to costs can be better understood by providing adequate context to the program improvements GAO has recommended in the past and that OPM has already implemented.

RECOMMENDATION 2: The Deputy Director for Management, Office of Management and Budget, in the capacity as Chair of the Performance Accountability Council, expand and specify reform related guidance to help ensure that reform stakeholders identify opportunities for cost savings, such as preventing duplication in the development of electronic case management and adjudication technologies in the suitability determination and personnel security clearance processes.

OPM RESPONSE:

See comment 5.

The GAO report recommendation to re-focus Government wide reform efforts on "improving cost savings" seems to miss the fact of reform benefits and large scale savings. Reform has a strategic focus on timeliness and quality - and through reform we have delivered the Executive Branch an estimated $24 billion in manpower productivity savings attributable solely to improvements in investigative timeliness since 2005. Reform's focus on "Alignment and Reciprocity" provide tremendous additional efficiencies beyond the $24 billion, with significant savings attributable to adjudicative timeliness and savings which as yet, are not fully measurable with regard to reciprocity. The progress and direction of reform have been repeatedly reinforced

5

by GAO, Congressional testimony and exchange, and in OMB publications to the White House
and Congress.

Although "direct cost savings" is a consideration in any reform activity (just as process fairness,
privacy protection, and information security are considerations) it was rightfully never intended
as a strategic goal. If we shift to prioritize immediate direct cost process savings at this point, we
run the risk of putting other strategic reform goals and deliverables in peril, along with the
associated incredible intangible/cost avoidance savings ($24 billion through investigative
timeliness improvements alone) and enhanced National Security "quality" benefits of "current"
reformed process.

The examples of "cost savings" failures cited by GAO as the basis for the "refocusing"
recommendation are not supported by all the facts. As the reform documentation demonstrates,
DoD CATS was not developed as the Reform enterprise solution. It was developed by DoD to
satisfy DoD unique requirements, and because the DoD is the largest adjudicative entity the
impact it has had on overall process timeliness has been significant. However, it is only one part
of a larger DoD enterprise system that provides full personnel management functions. Under
PAC leadership, the DoD CATS was demonstrated three times in Joint Reform forums and
during quarterly meetings, and was explored by a number of agencies. It is most portable to
agencies that have the same high volume consolidated processes; however, those agencies must
incorporate the DoD e-Adjudicate into their unique personnel management systems just as DoD
has done. Through these joint reform forums, the cost benefits analysis of incorporating the
DoD adjudication system into other agency operations was properly assessed by agencies, and
those that could benefit have already gone down that path. On the other hand, we have many
other demonstrated cost savings successes using these same reform forums. We made cost
benefits decisions to link OPM's Central Verification System with DoD's Joint Personnel
Adjudication System for maximum data sharing at limited expense, and when OPM provided
NSA the e-QIP system coding to build a "classified e-QIP system" at no cost to NSA. These
savings did not require a strategic cost saving goal to occur, and they did not put us off our
ultimate reform objectives.

Cost considerations are a part of each process reform and they will continue to be important
given current fiscal constraints. However, GAO's suggestion that focusing the PAC on IT
system "redundancy" will help ensure "cost savings" is not necessarily valid. The PAC's focus
on strategic reform goals have brought incredible intangible/cost avoidance and enhanced
National Security benefits that must remain the primary consideration. The PAC focus on cost
considerations is ultimately balanced by reform objectives and agency level cost benefit
assessments, which together create the reform implementation pathways forward.

Please contact Mr. Sean Hershey in Internal Oversight & Compliance 202-606-4175 if you
require additional information.

See comment 6.

See comment 7.

6

OPM appreciates the opportunity to respond to information in the draft report.

Sincerely,

John Berry
Director

The following are GAO's comments on specific points made in OPM's letter sent on January 24, 2012.

GAO Comments:

1. OPM stated that the GAO conclusions drawn from the OPM-provided information are often problematic and that the report does not always accurately interpret the information or clearly represent OPM information with appropriate balance. As stated in our report, we conducted this audit in accordance with government auditing standards, which require that we plan and perform the audit to obtain sufficient, appropriate evidence to provide a reasonable basis for our findings and conclusions based on our audit objectives. In addition, appendix I describes the scope and methodology used to carry out our work. We held meetings with and collected data from OPM officials as well as its executive branch agency customers and representatives from the Joint Reform Team. We sought to reflect all of those perspectives in our report to achieve balance.

2. OPM stated that this report provides direction that is inconsistent with many previous GAO recommendations. Further, OPM states that the reforms and improvements that explain the costs—congressionally mandated IRTPA timeliness requirements, elimination of the inherited DOD investigation backlog, workload shifts toward more costly fieldwork-intensive investigations, and delivery of suitability and security processes—were all recommended and endorsed by GAO over the years as necessary. We disagree. GAO has never made recommendations regarding elimination of the backlog, workload shifts, or merging suitability and security processes to the extent possible. Previous GAO recommendations regarding timeliness were to help ensure timeliness requirements outlined in statute were met. For example, in 2010 we recommended that the Chair of the Performance Accountability Council collaborate with executive branch agencies that were not meeting IRTPA timeliness objectives to identify the challenges and develop mitigation strategies, among other things.

3. Further, OPM stated that GAO creates many data scenarios to demonstrate cost increases throughout the report but does little to explain the reasons for the increases and to provide context to operating costs. We disagree. This report included both documented cost drivers and testimony from OPM officials regarding factors that contribute to increasing costs on page 15. Further, OPM was unable to provide documentation about how the factors it identified as "drivers," in its formal response increased operating costs.

4. OPM stated that GAO intentionally leaves information gaps and uses those gaps to support the recommendation that more transparency is needed. We disagree. As stated, we conducted this audit in accordance with government auditing standards, which require that we plan and perform the audit to obtain sufficient, appropriate evidence to provide a reasonable basis for our findings and conclusions based on our audit objectives. As stated on page 22, we found that OPM customer agencies do not understand the basis for OPM's investigation prices or the changes in prices, which led to the recommendation that OPM provide its customer agencies with more transparent information about prices. OPM agreed with this recommendation and stated that relating cost-benefits to its stakeholders is critical to its leadership role.

5. OPM commented on our recommendation to the Office of Management and Budget that the Deputy Director for Management, in the capacity as Chair of the Performance Accountability Council, help its reform partners identify continued administrative efficiencies and opportunities for cost savings. The Office of Management and Budget concurred with our recommendation and stated that it was pleased that this report assessed the cost of background investigations with respect to the larger scope of the ongoing governmentwide suitability and security clearance reform efforts. However, OPM stated that GAO overlooked the estimated $24 billion in productivity savings it has delivered the executive branch, attributable to the improvements in investigation timeliness. We disagree that this information was overlooked because OPM did not provide it during the course of our work, despite repeated requests for documentation of cost savings that resulted from the reform effort. OPM provided the cost savings estimate of $24 billion after reviewing a draft of this report. According to OPM officials, this estimate is based on productivity gained by OPM clearing the investigation backlog it inherited from DOD in the 2005 transfer. However, when we interviewed officials from the Office of Management, and Budget and the Joint Reform Team for this report, they were not able to provide documentation of cost savings resulting from the reform effort.

6. OPM stated that shifting the focus of the reform effort to direct costs savings would put other reform goals and deliverables in peril. We disagree. As previously stated, the overall mission statement of the governmentwide suitability and security clearance strategic framework includes cost efficiency. Therefore, it is GAO's interpretation that this mission should drive decisions at the strategic goal-level, and that of the reform effort's goals should be implemented with the whole mission, including cost efficiency, in mind. Further, none of the other reform leaders or stakeholders expressed concern that focusing on cost savings would put the reform effort in peril and the

Office of Management and Budget concurred with our recommendation to further expand and specify reform-related guidance to help ensure opportunities for cost savings are identified.

7. OPM stated that DOD's Case Adjudication Tracking System was not developed as the reform enterprise solution and that agencies interested in using CATS must have similar processes and incorporate the electronic adjudication module. In the report, we do not advocate the use of one case-management system. We encourage collaboration to prevent duplication in the development of multiple case-management systems that have similar capabilities. However, according to DOD officials, after the system was initially developed, the Department quickly realized its potential to be shared with other agencies. During the course of our work, DOD officials stated that their system is highly adaptable and that the electronic adjudication module of the Case Adjudication Tracking System can be turned on and off. Further, as stated in our report, the Department of Energy is piloting the system.

# Appendix V: Comments from the Department of Defense

Note: Page numbers in the draft report may differ from those in this report.

**OFFICE OF THE UNDER SECRETARY OF DEFENSE**
5000 DEFENSE PENTAGON
WASHINGTON, DC 20301-5000

JAN 2 4 2012

INTELLIGENCE

Ms. Brenda S. Farrell
Director
Defense Capabilities and Management
Government Accountability Office
Washington, DC 20548

Dear Ms. Farrell:

Thank you for the opportunity to review the draft report, GAO-12-197, "Background Investigations: Office of Personnel Management Needs to Improve Transparency of Its Pricing and Seek Cost Savings" (TAB B). The observations and recommendations detailed in the report provide sound justifications for pursuing greater efficiencies and costs savings for U.S. Office of Personnel Management customer agencies. The enclosure at TAB A provides feedback on sections of the report for your consideration. My point of contact for this effort is Mr. Timothy Davis, (703) 604-1219 or timothy.davis@osd.mil.

Sincerely,

Thomas A. Ferguson
Principal Deputy Under Secretary of Defense
for Intelligence

Enclosures:
As stated

## SUBSTANTIVE COMMENTS

### EMPHASIS ON CUSTOMER "COMPREHENSION" AS A SOURCE OF DISSATISFACTION

While further understanding of the prices is most definitely desired (coversheet, para 2), it should be understood that transparency may not result in concurrence with current pricing models. For many reasons, the DoD questions the justifications for the Office of Personnel Management's (OPM) prices, as outlined below.

### INCREASES IN OPM PRICES IN SPITE OF REPORTS OF GAINED EFFICIENCIES

The U.S. Government Accountability Office (GAO) report notes that OPM's income increased from about $602M in FY2005 to almost $1.1B in FY2010 and FY2011, representing average increases of over 10% each year, without a corresponding increase in average workload. The report caveats this reported increase by stating that dollar amounts may not be reliable due to material weaknesses in OPM's internal controls.

Regardless of the accuracy of the dollar amounts, the report reliably notes that OPM has implemented efficiencies which would reasonably be expected to result in cost savings to its customers. Recent changes, including automated database checks, electronic case files, and electronic delivery should have yielded great cost savings (fewer man hours, less ink and paper, and decreased delivery costs associated with overnighting thousands of paper investigations) yet none of these savings have been realized by DoD. OPM has failed to pass those cost savings to any of its customers. As examples:

- OPM has established a means to conduct most law enforcement agency checks, court records and creditor records from its center at Ft. Meade, Maryland, vice incurring costs for investigative agents to drive to local police departments, courts, or credit establishments across the country. In spite of the increased use of lower-cost automated checks, prices for investigations that rely heavily on these checks have increased.
- OPM and DoD began electronic delivery of completed investigative files in late 2009. Today, 98% of all DoD investigations are delivered electronically resulting in OPM no longer paying UPS to deliver the files. OPM has not passed this cost savings to DoD.
- As stated in the report, OPM has fixed price contracts with its investigative services contractors. It is DoD's understanding that in the fall of 2011, OPM renegotiated the prices of its investigative services contracts, requiring contractors to take a 15% price reduction. The cost savings was not passed along to OPM's customers, to include DoD.

1

- OPM states that the competition between the private investigation firms helps to keep
  costs down (page 8, para 1). OPM has no such competition in providing investigative
  services to federal customers, and consequently, DoD does not have competitive
  forces at work to drive DoD's costs down.

OPM claims they must continue to use a paper based system because only a small
number of their agencies have electronic capabilities (Page 29, para 1). DoD is one of the "few"
agencies that does have electronic capabilities and also represents 74% of the OPM workload. It
would certainly be more efficient for OPM to maintain an electronic system and then print out
the necessary files for agencies that are not capable of receiving them electronically than it is to
maintain everything in paper, and convert 74% or more to electronic formats.

## COSTS AND REQUIREMENTS FOR OPM IT

One of OPM's cost drivers is its information technology (IT) system (coversheet para 1,
page 12). In 2011, OPM invested $91M in technology improvements. DoD notes that OPM has
not contacted it, as its largest customer, to gather IT requirements. It is entirely possible that
OPM is investing in IT improvements that will fail to meet the customer agency needs. DoD
recommends that GAO require OPM to engage with DoD, as recipient of 75% of OPM's
workload (pg 1, pg 27), and ensure both organizations are developing IT improvements that will
be compatible. Note that OPM has increased expenditures on IT upgrades by 682% over a six
year period, without oversight by or negotiation with customer agencies.

In short, DoD does not want to finance technology upgrades by OPM that DoD has not
vetted and approved. For example, OPM is developing a system for purchase by smaller
agencies that cannot afford the $300,000 start-up cost of the Case Adjudication & Tracking
System in use by the DoD. OPM is doing so, however, using funds provided largely from DoD
to help cover the cost of development. In effect, this results in DoD funding development of a
system that the DoD will not use, with functionality that the DoD has already developed and
implemented to process OPM's case files.

## ACCURACY OF OPM's REPORTED PRICES AND PROBLEMS WITH OPM'S
## BILLING SYSTEM

DoD concurs that the Federal Investigations Notices (FIN) cover some of the costs
associated with the investigations (page 19, para 2), however, in addition to the most basic
investigation charge which is listed in the FIN, there are 24 additional transaction events billed to
DoD over the past two fiscal years. In fact, on the monthly bills received for investigations, only
55% of the transactions on the bill were for the investigations' published price while 45% of the
transactions were the unpublished, or little known add-ons, that OPM uses.

2

## RECIPROCITY

Reciprocity should not be an issue in using distributed investigation service providers (page 22-23, para 2). By establishing requirements, DoD and by extension the federal government at large, can dictate the nature of the product provided. By establishing standard requirements that must be adhered to, and even outlining the format for the investigations to be delivered, one can expect the same results, from multiple investigative providers, all while driving down the cost to the government. As an added benefit, technical requirements for delivery of investigative case files can contribute to greater efficiencies, cost-savings, and quality control in the adjudicative process than are currently possible using the OPM investigative product.

3

# Appendix VI: GAO Contact and Staff Acknowledgments

| GAO Contact | Brenda S. Farrell, (202) 512-3604 or farrellb@gao.gov |
| --- | --- |
| Staff Acknowledgments | In addition to the contact named above, Lori Atkinson (Assistant Director), Grace Coleman, Sara Cradic, Dianne Guensberg, Tara Jayant, Katherine Lenane, Jacqueline Nowicki, Charles Perdue, Tom Predmore, Jillena Roberts, Grant Sutton, and Michael Willems, made key contributions to this report. |

# Related GAO Products

*Intragovernmental Revolving Funds: Commerce Departmental and Census Working Capital Funds Should Better Reflect Key Operating Principles.* GAO-12-56. Washington, D.C.: November 18, 2011.

*Budget Issues: Better Fee Design Would Improve Federal Protective Service's and Federal Agencies' Planning and Budgeting for Security.* GAO-11-492. Washington, D.C.: May 20, 2011.

*High-Risk Series: An Update.* GAO-11-278. Washington, D.C.: February 16, 2011.

*Personnel Security Clearances: Overall Progress Has Been Made to Reform the Governmentwide Security Clearance Process.* GAO-11-232T. Washington, D.C.: December 1, 2010.

*Personnel Security Clearances: Progress Has Been Made to Improve Timeliness but Continued Oversight Is Needed to Sustain Momentum.* GAO-11-65. Washington, D.C.: November 19, 2010.

*DOD Personnel Clearances: Preliminary Observations on DOD's Progress on Addressing Timeliness and Quality Issues.* GAO-11-185T. Washington, D.C.: November 16, 2010.

*Intragovernmental Revolving Funds: NIST's Interagency Agreements and Workload Require Management Attention.* GAO-11-41. Washington, D.C.: October 20, 2010.

*Personnel Security Clearances: An Outcome-Focused Strategy and Comprehensive Reporting of Timeliness and Quality Would Provide Greater Visibility over the Clearance Process.* GAO-10-117T. Washington, D.C.: October 1, 2009.

*Personnel Security Clearances: Progress Has Been Made to Reduce Delays but Further Actions Are Needed to Enhance Quality and Sustain Reform Efforts.* GAO-09-684T. Washington, D.C.: September 15, 2009.

*Personnel Security Clearances: An Outcome-Focused Strategy Is Needed to Guide Implementation of the Reformed Clearance Process.* GAO-09-488. Washington, D.C.: May 19, 2009.

*DOD Personnel Clearances: Comprehensive Timeliness Reporting, Complete Clearance Documentation, and Quality Measures Are Needed to Further Improve the Clearance Process.* GAO-09-400. Washington, D.C.: May 19, 2009.

*High-Risk Series: An Update.* GAO-09-271. Washington, D.C.: January 2009.

*Personnel Security Clearances: Preliminary Observations on Joint Reform Efforts to Improve the Governmentwide Clearance Eligibility Process.* GAO-08-1050T. Washington, D.C.: July 30, 2008.

*Federal User Fees: A Design Guide.* GAO-08-386SP. Washington, D.C.: May 29, 2008.

*Personnel Clearances: Key Factors for Reforming the Security Clearance Process.* GAO-08-776T. Washington, D.C.: May 22, 2008.

*Employee Security: Implementation of Identification Cards and DOD's Personnel Security Clearance Program Need Improvement.* GAO-08-551T. Washington, D.C.: April 9, 2008.

*Personnel Clearances: Key Factors to Consider in Efforts to Reform Security Clearance Processes.* GAO-08-352T. Washington, D.C.: February 27, 2008.

*DOD Personnel Clearances: DOD Faces Multiple Challenges in Its Efforts to Improve Clearance Processes for Industry Personnel.* GAO-08-470T. Washington, D.C.: February 13, 2008.

*DOD Personnel Clearance: Improved Annual Reporting Would Enable More Informed Congressional Oversight.* GAO-08-350. Washington, D.C.: February 13, 2008.

*DOD Personnel Clearances: Delays and Inadequate Documentation Found for Industry Personnel.* GAO-07-842T. Washington, D.C.: May 17, 2007.

*High-Risk Series: An Update.* GAO-07-310. Washington, D.C.: January 2007.

*DOD Personnel Clearances: Additional OMB Actions Are Needed to Improve the Security Clearance Process.* GAO-06-1070. Washington, D.C.: September 28, 2006.

*DOD Personnel Clearances: New Concerns Slow Processing of Clearances for Industry Personnel.* GAO-06-748T. Washington, D.C.: May 17, 2006.

*DOD Personnel Clearances: Funding Challenges and Other Impediments Slow Clearances for Industry Personnel.* GAO-06-747T. Washington, D.C.: May 17, 2006.

*DOD Personnel Clearances: Government Plan Addresses Some Long-standing Problems with DOD's Program, But Concerns Remain.* GAO-06-233T. Washington, D.C.: November 9, 2005.

*A Glossary of Terms Used in the Federal Budget Process.* GAO-05-734SP. Washington, D.C.: September 2005.

*DOD Personnel Clearances: Some Progress Has Been Made but Hurdles Remain to Overcome the Challenges That Led to GAO's High-Risk Designation.* GAO-05-842T. Washington, D.C.: June 28, 2005.

*High-Risk Series: An Update.* GAO-05-207. Washington, D.C.: January 2005.

*OPM Revolving Fund: OPM Sets New Tuition Pricing Policy.* GAO/GGD-94-120. Washington, D.C.: April 6, 1994.

*OPM Revolving Fund: Investigation Activities During Fiscal Years 1983 Through 1986.* GAO/GGD-87-81. Washington, D.C.: June 26, 1987.

*OPM's Revolving Fund Policy Should Be Clarified and Management Controls Strengthened.* GAO/GGD-84-23. Washington, D.C.: October 13, 1983.